CHAKRA
HEALING

A Beginner's Guide to Self-Healing Techniques That Balance the Chakras

CONTENTS

■■■■■ ■■

INTRODUCTION

■ ■ ■ ■ ■ ■ ■

I pay good attention to everything that happens around me, especially at work. The moment my new patient, Ms. Juliet, walked into my office, I could clearly sense her disappointment with the state of things in her life presently. In fact, this also happens, whenever I am with a new patient. I listen carefully with what their Chakras have to say immediately they walk through my door.

The initial appointment for Ms. Juliet's was acupuncture treatment for stress and ankle pain. As a seasoned and licensed acupuncturist, I make use of Traditional Chinese Medicine. I started with feeling her pulse and reading her tongue to ascertain the health of her organs. As it is the case with most patients, it appeared what brought her here was deeper than a physical phenomenon. I figured that what she needed to alleviate was more than the complaint of stress and ankle pain from her job—even though she was yet to take note of it herself.

I was raised to be an empath; you might have possibly learnt that this is the root word of *empathy*. However, it is simply used to describe a person who can innately perceive the feelings of others, as if they feel the same way. I consider it to be such a remarkable gift. Just like others, at first, I took a while for me to understand what being an empath meant or how to embrace my intuitive gifts. People often dismissed me for being overly thoughtful or awkward. So, in an attempt to fit in, I eventually locked off that part of myself. Obviously, that seemed like the best thing to do, because that part of me was causing me troubles! I only needed an escape, and that was the only valid route to take. However, when we disconnect ourselves from who we are, our bodies tend to protest; they often become loud through emotional, mental, and or spiritual symptoms—until we pay good attention and fix them.

While Ms. Juliet and I talked about her medical health and other symptoms she was seeking treatment for, I figured that she was bearing fears within her. She eventually opened up about being creatively stuck at work, which she hated. One of her major ambitions is to become a yoga instructor and write about healing and holistic wellness, but she was scared to give it a push. She didn't trust her inner intuition, and was at the same time going through some distressing pains from her pasts—pains that currently stand as roadblocks to her goals.

With the use of acupuncture, Reiki, crystal work, and lots of compassion, Ms. Juliet's health eventually flourished and her emotional distress was gone. She began to allow herself to feel things genuinely unlike before, and this restored her creative prowess. This unique development set her on the direction of her dreams. She quit her job, finished up her yoga training and started freelancing for a wellness website. As we completed our treatments, her ankle pain was ameliorated. And, much later, she was only visiting for maintenance care.

Like Ms. Juliet, we are all capable of creating stories for ourselves—stories that inform how we live our lives. Some of them may be true; but, on the other hand, most of them are obsolete. What we do, oftentimes, is carrying the pain from these false stories into our energy centres, also known as *chakras*. It is important that we learn to be aware of what we carry in our individual energy systems; because, when we do so, we can deeply empower ourselves to become the radiant creatures we were meant to be. This is the ideal purpose of this book—to strongly make you aware of what you are carrying in your chakras, so you can be a genuine source of healing to yourself from inside.

If this is your first time to the world of chakras and energy healing, and you need basic guidelines to kick off, or, you are already deeply grounded on how the system works, and simply want to refresher on the basics, this book will help you on your healing journey, through understanding and care of your chakras.

1

THE
POWERFUL
CHAKRA
SYSTEM

In part 1, you will build your basic knowledge about the chakra system. Chapter 1 ushers you to the special qualities and powers of the seven main energy centres in your body; the idea is so you can understand the importance of keeping them balanced and free of blockages.

In chapter 2, you will learn about the various healing techniques which have been developed to ensure the health of the chakra system. Studying about these techniques could help you figure out the style or method that best suits you.

1

AN OVERVIEW
OF THE CHAKRAS

■■:■: ■■

In this chapter, I will make a basic introduction of the
chakra system– what they are, how to feel them, how
they operate, some myths and things to watch out for
about how chakra healing work, and, of course, how to
engage your healing centres safely. Also, others you will
learn in this chapter includes the individual
characteristics of each chakras, the possible causes for
energy blocks, and what happens to your physical,
emotional, mental, and spiritual health when your
chakras are in or out of harmony.

What Are Chakras?

I know that you are possibly familiar with your physical body. You already know how it feels to stretch or flex an area of your body; that your muscles are fixed to your bones; that your nerves signal to your limbs, torso and head; and that what you eat and drink directly affects your health. This gives you an idea of how aspects of your physical being are interconnected with each other, and how your five senses (touch, smell, taste, sight and hearing) informs each other, thereby creating your life experiences.

However, it is important to know that your physical body is not the only body you have. Whether what you are studying is chakra or quantum physics, you eventually realise that everything is basically made up of energy; each bearing its own vibrational frequency. From the littlest things like atoms that create our cells, organs, bones, muscles, and bodily systems to the biggest planet in the solar system, it all encompasses energy. The names of the energy have many names: qi, ki, chi, prana, mana, Odic force, bioplasm, and life force energy, among many others.

The energy body is a significant part of our existence. It is the human energy field that cuts across the physical body. Just the same way your body consists of many layers and systems, with inherent overlapping functions, that is how your body energy body is deeply wired to interconnect within. Each layer has a specific purpose and carries out its functions accordingly. Your energy body is collectively known as aura. This is what your aura does: it connects with the energy in your body, or chakras.

Chakra originates from *cakra*, a Sanskrit word that simply means "wheel." History reveals that it was first mentioned in the Vedas, ancient Hindu texts that date to around 1,500 BCE. The chakra history has been widely known across diverse cultures to be a situation that reflects the natural law that exists within the universe and the mixed counterpart of our physical bodies. Such cultures include that of the Egyptians, Chinese, Hindus, Greeks, Native Americans, Incas, Zarathustrians, Sufis and many others.

Chakras are simply channels of energy that our embedded in our innermost beings. These channels are responsible for discreetly transporting energy from the universe around you into the aura and body, and even your physical body. Comparing this situation with how the bloodstream works will definitely help us understand it better. For example, in our system, the blood carries oxygen, nutrients and hormones throughout the body; the idea is to ensure that the body is in a balanced state of health through constant regulation, removing waste products and quickly clotting when it is harmed. Essentially, the same way the bloodstream is connected to and helps your body, this is also how your chakra plays a unique role as a vital support system to your physical self and energy self in diverse ways.

Interestingly, every living thing on earth has a chakra system—animals, trees, plants and humans. A channel of energy distribution embedded in their beings. These chakras in the body are divided into two: the major and minor. In fact, each of them has their specific roles they perform while connected to a particular organs, glands, physical functions and dysfunctions, and emotional, mental and spiritual issues. We will look into more detailed information on them as we go further in this chapter.

Our chakras are one of our greatest possessions as human beings. It is simply amazing to know how much we can do with them. In fact, when we begin to get in touch with our chakras, we learn to connect to ourselves more fully, thereby teaching ourselves whole healing. It stabilizes the body and mind into a state of calmness and peace. Also, mindfulness-based such as yoga, meditation etc. are important and strongly recommended, because they help us connect with our mind and body. The beautiful thing about this is when our spirit is nurtured; it eventually heals our minds and bodies.

They are all connected.

FEEL YOUR CHAKRAS

If you want to get in touch with your energy, this is actually how to go about it. Firstly, raise your hands one inch apart and ensure that both palms are facing each other. Familiarise yourself with the sublime energy and warmth exchange that flow between your hands. (Our hands contain minor chakras). Now slightly separate your hands, as you stretch the energy embedded between your palms. Then bring them closer again in an attempt to condense your energy. You might want to repeat these a few times after. As you do these, don't worry, if you don't seem to perceive or feel anything yet. Just relax your mind, with the thought that you are in touch with your chakra.

As you are gradually getting used to your energy, your sensitivity sharpens in the process. In fact, you will sharply notice the growing warmth of your hands and the slight exchange of energy between them. With patience and consistency, this feeling will intensify and you will begin to feel it more strongly; even, when your hands are widely separated.

However, it is possible to feel your major chakras, too. If you want to feel your heart chakra, rest both hands at the centre of your chest. Inhale gently. Try to feel the warm and glow of life under your hands. As you do this, you will not only begin to feel your pulse, your heart beat and blood coursing through your veins; but, also the sense how your heart chakra expands.

I guess you can now feel it, right? Congratulations! Well done as you are now getting connected to your chakras. It is okay, if you are yet to feel anything. Your sensitivity will increase as you practice, over time, with patience and consistency.

The Power of Chakras to Heal

It has been said that the knowledge involved in the chakras for healing and enlightenment is ancient wisdom; this wisdom has been popularly used in lots of ancient cultures for centuries. The growing interest in chakras is simply because we are beginning to be largely disposed to being more sensitive to many things to the point that treating only our physical health is not enough to heal us completely. Regardless of the many milestones in medicine, there seems to be something vital that we cannot particularly point out or identify.

Having grown up as a doctor's child, in the Western world, I am privileged to be fully aware of the level of contributions being been made to healthcare by Western medicine, and I truly appreciate it. I grew up watching my Dad take care of his patients with kindness and astute regard. I often ran into his medical notes, texts and read his references. This made me realise how amazing the human body actually is. However, people are gradually taking note of it; but, even if they don't understand it yet, the fact remains that there are factors that are capable of influencing our health challenges.

Apart from accidents or other physical impacts that come through direct trauma, do you know that many other physical symptoms that we experience?

Enter the chakras.

The health of our body system is greatly determined by the state of our chakras. Our health will be good, when our chakras are in balance. In the same vein, our lives will flourish in complete harmony, too.

I have stated earlier that everything in life revolves around energy. It is important that we are intentional in our approach towards maintaining the energy of our body's health. Such can be actualized through effective modalities, like acupuncture, yoga, qi gong, Reiki, meditation, adopting a healthy lifestyle and eating healthy. When we do these, we hinder chances of being plagued by some sort of sickness. Also, it gets to help us take care of certain health issues before they manifest physically.

MYTHS ABOUT CHAKRA

Before we delve into the chakra system, it is important that we clarify some myths for which chakra have been long known.

Myth 1: *Chakra healing is an outside job*

It is actually natural to think that chakra healing is an outside job simply because you go out to meet a practitioner in his facility, who eventually takes you down the process.

Oh, yes! It is.

However, it does not matter where one receives his or her chakra healing; because, at the end of the day, the healing that you seek comes from deep within you. This is an information that every patient or intending patient need to know. This misconception have shaped people's mental picture about chakra to the point that the process turns out difficult for them, simply because they relied on their practitioners to heal them. No, that is wrong. While it is the job of healing practitioners to guide us in this venture, our role is to bring the healing we seek to ourselves.

Myth2: *Chakra healing is affiliated with a specific religion.*

It is true that chakra healing system of practices has it's originates from religious texts and relics, and used to be popularly dominated by such. However, this notion had since greatly evolved to be embraced by people from many walks of life. Many people are beginning to see the ultimate role that chakra plays in contributing to our wellbeing and overall health.

Myth 3*: Chakra healing is a form of demonic or dark, ritual*

The negative notion of darkness or evil attributed to chakra is simply an attempt to define it by those who did not understand it. Truly, chakra is simply a pure effort to achieve wellness. In fact, it is the opposite of demonic. When done well, light, peace, consciousness and awareness are infused into your heart, body, soul and spirit. It does not harbour it; instead, it dispels it.

CHAKRA HEALING WARNINGS

There are a good number of things that you should bear in mind as you begin to engage with healing your chakras:

Patience:

It is really natural to lose patience, when beginners are trying to get in touch with their chakras. I observe it a lot as a guide my trainees in their respective journeys. The common thing they share is simply their inability to persevere through the entire process, especially in situations, where. In other words, they lose patience quickly. It is important to note that everyone is not on the same path in this venture; and, although they may have a common focus, they will have unique experiences in due time. It is important to note that chakra healing is simply an intentional attempt geared towards self-exploration and not a goal. It is not a goal, because it is something that anyone can achieve in a hurry. It requires patience. On the other hand, chakra healing restores or aligns our energy centres together after getting rid of obstacles that tear them apart.

Do not push yourself too hard:

One common experience that people have while trying to connect with their chakras is pushing so hard that they are almost get hurt in the process. This is unhealthy as it could deter you from reaching the main goal. So, whenever you begin to get stressed, take a break.

Seek help from a healing practitioner when necessary:

There is a lot that can be achieved when you set out you your own; but, sometimes, it is needful to involve the guidance and counsels of a seasoned, who will guide you on areas that do not seem to be an easy ride. This is important, because it will greatly contribute to your overall success in this venture. Also, when you eventually set out to hire the services of a healing practitioner, make sure that the person is licensed and officially certified as stated. Ensure that he or she is good, kind and friendly.

Chakra Basics

The chakra system is basically rooted in seven major chakras within our body. They are collectively linked and serve a common purpose in the body.

The three upper layers are known as the spiritual chakras. This basically focuses on how we connect to the Divine, and, of course, our Higher Self; it is the version of ourselves that is tapped into most genuine form of love, wisdom and power. The three lower layers of the chakras are known as the physical chakras. They help us get anchored on earth as human beings. As a matter of fact, the heart chakras play a key role as it is the medium through which the physical and spiritual chakras are both connected in the centre.

ACTIVATING YOUR KUNDALINI ENERGY

Kudalini energy is the basically the solid, illuminating force that prompts all your chakras to life almost simultaneously. The fact is that we all inherently have massive energy within us; but, it is often dormant and quietly laid, like a lion at rest at the base of the spine also known as the root chakra.

It is common knowledge that this kudalini energy can be awakened, when working with the chakras. And, it is true, because when we begin to open our chakras, there is a great possibility that it would happen. However, there is no guarantee that this would happen suddenly, especially reading it up in a book or after trying out a couple of chakra healing techniques. In fact, it takes a while for such to happen, and it is particularly in cases of people, who have consistently cultivated it in their lives over time either by continually receiving energy work or practising kudalini yoga.

Kudalini energy is not really a hard nut to crack. In fact, when it is done with due circumspection and ease, the outcome promises to be one full of joy, agility, heightened sensitivity and full consciousness. This is why those who are seeking for enlightenment often make efforts to achieve it through various practices such as mindfulness exercises, meditation and kudalini yoga.

On the other hand, if the kudalini comes alive through yoga or other possible means, while you are not fully prepared for it, the energy could get stuck. Due the massive energy shooting through your body, you will have symptoms of physical pain and such will not be easy to manage. It is so serious that these outcomes could be intense in some cases. In fact, some people might experience trauma or emotional instability. This is why it is important that you understand how this process works to enable you make necessary adjustments as the situation demands. So when your kudalini energy gets prompted to life, and you are not prepared, quickly seek the attention and guidance of a good spiritual teacher.

More so, there are other ways to activate your chakra apart from summoning your kudalini energy; although the practice of kudalini has been on for a very long time. However, the alternative ways to activating your chakra are characteristically full of calmness and ease.

THE ROOT CHAKRA

The root chakra is actually the foremost physical chakras; that is, the one responsible for making you feel safe.

When the Root Chakra is not in Alignment

Everything ceases to be in place, when the root chakra is out of harmony. At this point, there is a tendency not to trust nature anymore. It also comes with a disturbing anxiety that makes us disconnected from the natural flow of the universe. We feel unsafe, have trust issues with friends and strangers, criticise our tribal and cultural beliefs, feel threatened and insecure of the fact that we are enough and have all that we need.

When the Root Chakra is in Harmony

It is always a breath of fresh air, when the root chakra is in alignment. We are well grounded and connected. There is a sense of ease and understanding in how we relate and approach the things and people around us, especially family, friends, strangers, cultural and tribal beliefs etc. We feel safe, secured and trust in the abiding providence of nature.

SANSKRIT
Muladhara

OTHER NAMES
Base chakra, first chakra

LOCATION
Right between the genitals and the anus, base of spine

COLOUR
Red

ELEMENT
Earth

AFFIRMATION
"I am"

PHYSICAL DYSFUNCTION
constipation, sciatica, varicose veins, rectal tumours or cancer, obese problems, anxiety, arthritis, knee pain, intense lower back pain, immune related illness

MENTAL/EMOTIONAL ISSUES
The security of the group and physical family, being able to feed oneself and for the family.

POSSIBLE CAUSES OF ENERGY BLOCKS
Guilt, anxiety, depression, fear of being alive

CRYSTALS
Ruby, fire agate, lodestone, smoky quartz, hematite, obsidian, black onyx, red jasper, black tourmaline, bloodstone

ESSENTIAL OILS
Vetiver, patchouli, sandalwood, Myrrh, spikenard

GLANDS
Adrenals

PHYSICAL BODY PARTS
Here we have the teeth, bones,
legs, physical body, base of
spine, immune system,
large intestine, feet

LIFE LESSON

To feel peaceful and secured
 in the universe, to provide our
basic needs and to be able to
cultivate healthy (physical)
sexuality.

THE SACRAL PLEXUS CHAKRA

The sacral plexus chakra is the second chakra. It is located directly above the root chakra. Just like the root chakra is responsible for making you feel safe, this chakra is closely connected with our emotions and creative activities, and of course, sexual and reproductive emotions.

When the Sacral Plexus Chakra is out of Alignment

Whenever the sacral plexus chakra is out of harmony, there turns out to be a state of emotional instability in the life of the individual. For instance, there is difficulty in expressing how we feel at certain times, especially in situations that are closely related to pleasure, joy and anger. Our creative prowess withers as we stifle our instincts, and in turn, blame ourselves for not being able to come up with creative or innovative ideas.

On the other hand, we also tend to have issues in our relationships, sexual lives, and even our self-worth. There is this tendency to feel shameful about who and where we are. This also extends to our finances, especially as regards property acquisitions: to have or not to have, that is the question.

When the Sacral Plexus Chakra is in Alignment

In this phase, everything becomes as smooth as it should be. We are right at the core of our creative prowess, flowing with precision, coming up with ideas and at ease with our feelings. There is no difficulty in expressing oneself as desired. The ease is present and nourishing, helping us to approach our relationships and sexuality with understanding. We have a balanced self-esteem and lack pressure as regards wealth and abundance, with willingness to grow from step to step.

SANSKRIT NAME
Svadisthana

OTHER NAMES
Pelvic chakra, naval chakra,
second chakra, sacral chakra

LOCATION
Two inches below the navel

COLOUR
Orange

ELEMENT
Water

AFFIRMATION
"I feel"

GLANDS
Ovaries, testicles

PHYSICAL BODY PARTS
Womb, genitals, hip, bladder,
pelvis, lower vertebrae,
appendix, kidneys

LIFE LESSON
To connect to others emotionally
without having to lose our
true selves,
to be freely creative,
and live with emotional stability

PHYSICAL DYSFUNCTION
Pelvic pain, sciatica,
impotence, uterine/bladder/kidney
problems, chronic lower back
pains, gynaecological problems

MENTAL/EMOTIONAL ISSUES
Sex, guilt, anxiety, depression, blame,
money, power and control, fame,
creativity

**POSSIBLE CAUSES OF ENERGY
BLOCKS**
depression, trauma, rape or sexual
abuse

CRYSTALS
Carnelcoral, orange tourmaline,
moonstone, coral, sunstone

ESSENTIAL OILS
Yiang yiang, lemon, sandalwood,
rosewood, patchouli

THE SOLAR PLEXUS CHAKRA

The solar plexus chakra is located right above the sacral plexus chakra. This unique chakra is the one that deeply connects with our whole existence and how we perceive ourselves; that is, our self-esteem, self-worth and personality.

When the Solar Plexus Chakra is out of Alignment

In this phase of existence, we are anxious or pressured to prove ourselves, no matter how small in order to feel good. We are contented; therefore, we want to massage our egos by craving attention, keeping up appearances and being recognised on the spotlight. Also, we give away our power too much by letting things get to us; and, although we may not respect ourselves too much, it is replaced with self-hatred and little or no significant self-esteem.

When the Solar Plexus Chakra is in Alignment

When our solar plexus chakra is in harmony, we operate from a place of peace, wholeness and strength. We are not pressured to prove anything to anyone. We are tune with who we are, including our strengths and weaknesses, while tolerating what does not look like it. We lack anxiety, but rather calm, peaceful and happy.

SANKRIT NAME
Manipura

OTHER NAMES
Power chakra, third chakra

LOCATION
Two inches above the navel

COLOUR
Yellow

ELEMENT
Fire

AFFIRMATION
"I can"

GLANDS
Pancreas, adrenals

PHYSICAL BODY PARTS
Middle spine, stomach,
upper intestines, liver,
gall bladder, spleen

LIFE LESSON
To deeply get in tune and
experience who we are with
self-esteem and self-empowerment,
to live and maximise our the purpose
of our life's or soul's existence

PHYSICAL DYSFUNCTION
hepatitis, anorexia or bulimer,
gastric or duodenal ulcers,
liver or adrenal dysfunction, chronic
or acute indigestion, fatigue, colon/
intestinal problems, pancreatic/diabetes

MENTAL/EMOTIONAL ISSUES
self-confidence, self-esteem, trust, fear,
anxiety, lack of contentment, personal
honour, sensitivity to criticism, care of
self and others, responsibility for
making decisions, trust

POSSIBLE CAUSES OF ENERGY BLOCKS
depression, trauma, rape or sexual
abuse

CRYSTALS
Rutilated quartz, yellow agate, yellow
topaz, yellow tiger's eye, yellow citrine,
amber

ESSENTIAL OILS
Rosemary, rosewood, lemon, lavender,
Roman chamolie

THE HEART CHAKRA

The heart is one of the most unique of all the chakras. This is because anything that has to do with the heart gives us a touch of experience that is beyond the realm we can see. In fact, it ultimately connects both the physical and spiritual aspects of our lives. The beauty of it is not just that it binds the physical and spiritual chakras, it is provides an avenue where we can relate with the world through connecting with our Higher Self.

When the Heart Chakra is out of Alignment

In this phase, we are thoroughly disconnected from our true selves, making us to approach things from a place of anxiety, hurt and low self-worth. We feel undeserving of care, love and attention. More so, we think that we are not worthy to love ourselves and love others, too. Here, the depression develops from being disconnected from ourselves over time.

When the Heart Chakra is in Alignment

Here, everything is in place as it ought to be. When we are fully connected to our true selves, we become at peace with the world in such a way that we flow from a place of ease. We are easily joyful, loving and accepting ourselves, while doing the same to others with contentment, gratitude and understanding.

SANSKRIT NAME
Anahata

OTHER NAMES
Fourth chakra

LOCATION
At the middle of the chest

COLOUR
Green

ELEMENT
Air

AFFIRMATION
"I love"

GLANDS
Thymus

PHYSICAL BODY PARTS
Heart, lungs, ribs,
breasts, diaphragm, arms
circulatory system,
pericardium, shoulders

LIFE LESSON
To strive towards being
compassionate while dealing
with ourselves and others.

PHYSICAL DYSFUNCTION
Lung disease, lung cancer, bronchial
pneumonia, high blood pressure,
 asthma/allergies, congestive heart
failure, heart attack

MENTAL/EMOTIONAL ISSUES
Hope, trust, forgiveness, compassion,
loneliness, resentment, grief, love
and hatred,

POSSIBLE CAUSES OF ENERGY
Stifled heartaches, grief, depression

CRYSTALS
Peridot, jade, green tourmaline,
emerald, green kyanite,
green calcite, rose quartz,

ESSENTIALS OILS
Palmarosa, geranium, lavender,
yiang yiang, bergamont, Rose,
neroli

THE THROAT CHAKRA

The throat chakra falls among the first of the spiritual chakras. And, one unique thing about it is that it has to do with our real voice, where understanding and faith come together.

When the Throat Chakra is out of Alignment

When the throat chakra is out of alignment, things automatically cease to flow accordingly. We experience difficulties in speaking out truths that deeply align with our cores, thereby expressing ourselves falsely. Also, we feel judged, misunderstood, silenced and lacking zeal to live our lives as we ought to.

When the Throat Chakra is in Alignment

In this phase, life becomes a breath of fresh air. We are filled with a strong zeal to live and chase after our dreams to the fullest. As opposed to the when it is not in harmony, we are full of life and power. We are confident in ourselves to speak our truths, which includes saying what we mean and meaning it. We are authentic and open in how we express ourselves creatively, without holding anything back.

SANSKRIT NAME
Vishuddha

OTHER NAMES
Fifth chakra

LOCATION
At the middle of the chest

COLOUR
Light blue

ELEMENT
Sound

AFFIRMATION
"I speak"

AFFIRMATION
"I speak"

GLANDS
Thyroid, parathyroid

PHYSICAL BODY PARTS

Hands, arms, mouth

PHYSICAL DYSFUNCTION
Gum difficulties, TMJ, stiff neck, swollen glands, mouth ulcers, scoliosis, raspy or sore throat, thyroid problems

MENTAL/EMOTIONAL ISSUES
Personal expression, strength of will, faith, addiction, judgement, following one's dream, criticisms, choice and capacity to make decisions, strength of will, creativity

POSSIBLE CAUSES OF ENERGY BLOCKS

Inability to express oneself, holding back or reserving words, suppressing creative talents

CRYSTALS
lapis lazuli, celestite, blue kyanite, turquoise, soladite aquamarine

ESSENTIALS OILS
Rosemary, lavender, German chamolie, frankincense, hyssop

teeth and gums, esophagus
throat, trachea, neck vertebrae,
shoulders, hypothalamus

LIFE LESSON
To always speak and receive the Truth.

THE THIRD EYE CHAKRA

The Third Eye chakra is the sixth chakra, which is also linked to "our sixth sense". Our sixth is the space where our intuition, wisdom and spiritual insight are accommodated.

When the Third Eye Chakra is out of Alignment

When the third eye chakra is out of alignment, we appear to be only mindful or connected to only what goes on in this realm, while neglecting the potentials of our spirituality. The refusal to see beyond our physical realities is mainly marked by fear of failure or fear of being misled by our inner wisdom.

When the Third Eye Chakra is in Alignment

When the third eye chakra is in alignment, we operate differently as opposed to when it is not. In this phase, we are highly aware of how our lives play out from day to day. Our plans and decisions are not only determined by the realities we can see; rather we operate as spiritual beings, seeing and envisioning realities beyond this realm. In fact, we trust our intuition to guide us and direct us.

SANSKRIT NAME
Ajna

OTHER NAMES
Brow chakra,
Sixth chakra,
forehead chakra

LOCATION
Between the eyebrows

COLOUR
Indigo

ELEMENT
Light

AFFIRMATION
"I see"

GLANDS
Pineal

PHYSICAL DYSFUNCTION
blurred vision, deafness, seizures,
headaches, disabilities, stroke,
spinal difficulties, neurological
disturbances, brain tumor/haemorrhage

MENTAL/EMOTIONAL ISSUES
self-evaluation, low self-esteem,
being open to others' ideas, truth,
intellectual abilities, learning from
experiences, emotional intelligence

POSSIBLE CAUSES OF ENERGY
Distrust for one's intuition

CRYSTALS
kyanite, tanzanite, fluorite,
star sapphire, clear quartz, sugilite,
lepidolite, amethyst, lapis lazuli,

ESSENTIALS OILS
Sandalwood, frankincense, lavender

PHYSICAL BODY PARTS
Nervous systems, eyes, nose,
ears, brains

LIFE LESSON
To see beyond the physical with the use of
insight and intuition

THE CROWN CHAKRA

The very last of the chakras is a unique as it plays a major role by being the source of connection source to the divine and our higher selves. It is called the crown chakra.

When the Crown Chakra is out of Alignment

Being out of harmony with our crown chakra is synonymous to being disconnected from the divinity and the spiritual source of our livelihood here on earth. We get angry at God for reasons we cannot clearly express. We lack confidence in our journeys. Life becomes a rollercoaster of negativities coming right after us, and leaving us deep with anxiety, depression and fear.

When the Crown Chakra is in Alignment

In this phase, we walk with the knowledge that we are connected uniformly. We are aware of how our connection with the divine reflects on our daily living, and capitalise on that to make the best of our existence here on earth. We believe that we are not just physical beings, but embody supernatural qualities capable of breaking physical strongholds. We are at peace with the world and ourselves; happy, confident and graceful.

SANSKRIT NAME
Sahasrara

OTHER NAMES
Seventh chakra

LOCATION
At the top and centre
of the head

COLOUR
Gold, white,
purple

ELEMENT
Thought

AFFIRMATION
"I know"

GLANDS
Pituitary

PHYSICAL BODY PARTS
Nervous systems, eyes, nose,
ears, brains

LIFE LESSON
To whole live and experience
the divine life

PHYSICAL DYSFUNCTION
Apathy, alienation, confusion,
energetic disorders, depression,
confusion, sensitivity to light/sound/
other factors in the environment, chronic
fatigue

MENTAL/EMOTIONAL ISSUES
Devotion, faith, spirituality, courage
values, ethics, selflessness, ability to
trust life and the divine, lacking
foresight, inspiration

POSSIBLE CAUSES OF ENERGY
Distrust towards the Divine or life,
perpetual anger towards the Divine

CRYSTALS
White topaz, kunzite, moonstone,
phenacite, apophyllite, Herkimer,
diamond, labradorite, clear quartz
amethyst, selenite

ESSENTIALS OILS
Sandalwood, frankincense, peppermint,
lotus

2

WORKING WITH
THE CHAKRAS

∎∎∙∙∎ ∙∎∎

In this chapter, we will be elaborately looking at the most available, common methods that are used by practitioners to harness chakra power and how they work. On the other hand, I will share recommendations that border on when to receive an acupuncture or Reiki treatment to facilitate proper healing of the chakras. Also, I will share pieces of advice cum tips that will help you maintain a balanced chakra system and create a discreet healing space wherever you are; office, home etc.

Harnessing Your Chakra Power

Our chakras are core parts of us. In order to heal or keep them in harmony, it is important that we are aware of the methods required to do so. There are a handful of various ways or methods that we can use to heal our chakras. They include using crystals and essential oils, practicing yoga, changing old habits, visualizations and meditations, and eating healthy. However, various healing techniques are covered here because different people make use of the ones that they are drawn. In order to get the best outcome, I encourage my patients to keep using the ones that they love, since none, of the technique, is necessarily better than the other.

Nevertheless, it is important that there are methods that are considerably best to start with so as to give you the accurate healing you deserve. If your problem has to do with your mental health or matters of the heart, I recommend you begin with meditation, crystal work or essential oils. If it is related to physical problems, you might want to change your diet. Sign up for yoga classes; get acupuncture, massage and other work outs.

MEDITATION AND VISUALIZATIONS

Meditation is a unique form of practice which involves training the mind on how stay relaxed and focus on a particular course, goal or sensation, like your breath.

Purpose

When the mind is in a turbulent state, the best way to calm the tension is by meditating. It stabilises our mental health in no small way. However, regular meditation goes a long way to transform to heal the conscious state of mind in a way that brings about peace, emotional positivity, clarity, mental strength, insight and focus, and allows us to regain our grounds, when we feel distraught. Tools that help you maintain focus during meditation includes: reciting a mantra, your breath, looking at a specific physical object etc. Without these, the mind will continue to wander and get lost in thoughts. Visualization is also part of meditation which involves creating a mental image or picture that is related to a specific purpose. One good way to connect to a chakra is by envisioning the colours or flows that are tied to it.

A healthy advantage of meditation is that it helps us to control how we react to our emotions, especially the upsetting ones. During meditation, you are required to keep your focus, without judging any distracting feeling or thought that comes across your mind. This skill helps us to be in better control of our emotions. It is simply known as mindfulness. When practiced very well, mindfulness can actually serve as an effective tool for cultivating peace, stability, calmness and compassion in our daily lives. For the purpose of this book, you can utilise its advantages to connect and strengthen your chakras. Meditation equally serves as an effective tool and medium that will help you stay connected with your energy and physical bodies.

How It Is Implemented

Meditation is not a one-way exercise. In fact, there are various ways in which meditation can be practiced, without losing its effectiveness. You can do it while journaling, playing music, walking, painting, eating etc. Also, the time frame differs for everyone. While some people practice for five to ten minutes, others prefer to go on for a longer period of time; and, that is okay, provided that everyone is fulfilled at the end of the day. In part two of this book, we will be looking at various meditation exercises that are unique to different chakras. These techniques are special to them, because they help to heal them. Do not worry about the time frame, because most will not require longer than five to ten minutes.

Why/How It Works

The practice of meditation is globally recognised. Having endured the test of time, its origin can be traced to centuries. This is basically so, because of its unique role in our minds. We all get to that point where we want to cultivate habits that will help us relax or quieten our minds, and retain our focus amidst a bustling society and busy daily routines. According to a 2016 study carried out in *Consciousness and Cognition* reveals that a session of meditation has the power to reduce physiological symptoms of anger, regardless if the meditator is a beginner or seasoned.

Pros/Cons of Using This Method

Pros: On a good note, it is important to know that meditation can be practiced anywhere, anytime and within any time frame. It relaxes our minds in order to cultivate genuine mental strength and focus. It helps us connect to our deepest selves that it is easier to navigate into higher realms. Meditation also creates an avenue that makes self-healing easier, and equally mindfulness from which we can largely experience the peace that comes with it.

Cons: There is a term used to describe optimal distraction that is known as "monkey mind." This is a situation where the mind wanders off on its own accord to God-knows-where. This is what the experience will look like during meditation: you mind will wander away, drifting your attention things, like bills, taxes, pending tasks, etc. Hey, don't worry, because even the best of meditators experience this, too.

Meditation is regarded as "a practice", because of its unique way of training the mind to settle into a state of deep awareness and focus. To achieve this, consistency is required. No one ever became a great meditator in a day.

CHANGING OLD HABITS

Success in life is highly determined by our ability to cultivate and work with the right habits. The same principle applies to our chakras, which appear to be in an imbalanced state as a result of a number of bad habits that we are yet to get rid. The key to restore and heal our chakras is by making efforts to cultivate new, healthy habits.

Purpose

The purpose of this venture is to ensure that we are transformed into people with a new, but different thought patters that will guide us to achieve the needed goal. As a matter of fact, our chakras are best healed when we re-evaluate how we think and interact with others in the society.

How It's Implemented

Usually, the first step is realised by making the people aware of what they have been doing wrongly, and definitely how to make it right. This includes outlining the various bad habits that are toxic to our chakras. When they become aware, they will definitely take steps to change them as soon as possible.

Some examples of such toxic habits include; remaining in an abusive relationship with a violent partner. A good way to go about this is to seek counsel on how to call it quit; talk to a reliable friend or support groups that will give you the comfort that you need; and equally help you to heal well enough to cope in subsequent relationships.

Another example is noticing that you cannot express yourself effectively; that is, you choose to keep quiet and stay suppressed about everything that happens to you. This could indicate an imbalance in your throat chakra. The best step to take, in this venture, is to brainstorm ways that will propel you to react different to things and scenarios. It could be leaving your immediate environment, connecting with a partner that loves to hear your thoughts, and joining support groups where everyone is expected to share their life's experiences.

Breaking the barriers of old and unhelpful habits is not a walk in the park. Instead, it will require constant patience, dedication and commitment. However, doing so creates the change that enables us get to where we want to be.

Why/How It Works

It actually works, because when we are intentionally concerned about altering problematic behavioural patterns for positive changes, we eventually come up with solutions that are needed to make them happen. It is achieved by practicing enough; doing this makes room for those wrong beliefs and patterns to cease to exist.

Pros/Cons of Using This Method

Pros: This method really works. Change is constant and when we replace old habits with new, healthy habits makes us positive and yields results.

Cons: It takes a long time as well as constant repetitions before one gets used to the patterns.

YOGA

There are numerous forms of yoga that are being recognised and practiced all over the world; but, the one that is mostly practiced is called *asama.* It is actually a series of breathing exercises and physical postures aimed at equipping us spiritually, mentally and spiritually.

Purpose

Asana is a program under yoga that sees to effective bodily exercise and postures that allow us develop the strength, stamina, awareness and connection throughout the body. In fact, it stands out as an effective tool for personal development on various levels; mentally, physically and spiritually.

How It's Implemented

There are a handful of ways through which the body and mind can be connected; but physical exercise and breath is an effective way to go about it. By doing so, the mind gets connected with the tissues in our body. In this venture, it is important to know the postures that are responsible for restoring balance and awareness to every particular chakra. As we practice yoga asana, we move the body to different postures and hold still for particular periods of time, before switching to the next. While holding still, we control our breath, so as to allow our energy to flow through every fibre of our being by cultivating mindfulness. When it comes to balancing chakras, different styles of yoga are very useful. One of them is Kudalini yoga, which achieves its purpose through physical poses, chanting, breathing techniques, and meditation to reinvigorate the Kudalini energy which in turn, permeates through our chakras.

However, it is important to note that while accommodating the idea of a yoga plan, there are more advanced yoga postures which pose to be of high risk injury in this venture. As a result, they should be taken with caution. For instance, head-stand and shoulder-stand are not advisable for anyone with neck or shoulder injury. If the person insists, it has to be done under the watch and guidance of a trained yoga instructor.

Why/How It Works

One powerful role that yoga plays is that it helps to reinvigorate enormous life force into the chakras, creating awareness and opening the chakras. Generally, it aids in taking down our bodies through a path that gives them a discreet sensory experience. This is particularly useful to people who have been deeply withdrawn into themselves–heads and bodies; but, largely disconnected from the energy of the world and its concreteness. This also reveals that our posture reflects how we move with the world.

For instance, when we are goofy and happy, our postures are not affected, because we are at ease and alright. However, an experience, like grief makes us droop our shoulders, while we are lost in thoughts. This goes ahead to create a concave movement with our bodies, which is a natural attempt to protect our heart chakras. But, keeping this posture for quite a long time could create physical problems in the shoulders, waist and upper back regions. What yoga does is to make us aware of these affected areas and as engage it while practicing, we eventually, ultimately release it.

Pros/Cons of Using This Method

Pros: Yoga is popularly practiced around the world today, because of the numerous healthy benefits accrued to it–physically, spiritually and mentally. It is an excellent type of exercise, even though it requires a lot of physical movement. Its practices can be carried anywhere, and does not require expensive instruments. However, instructors prefer to hold their classes in serene studios or nature-friendly environments, because they are warmly soothing and beneficial for wellness. Since yoga helps us to cultivate awareness or sensitivity, some people have capitalised on this advantage to improve the quality of their lives, this ranges from practicing healthy eating to more quality lifestyles.

Cons: The fees of yoga classes are not static, and in some regions, they can be as expensive as possible. Also, not everyone has the luxury of creating time for it. On the other hand, with a plethora of tutorial videos online, yoga practice might be challenging for a beginner, because he or she direly needs a physical instructor at that stage; this especially has to do with ensuring that the learner is getting all the postures and following other pertinent instructions properly.

Nevertheless, practicing yoga is not an easy road. While some people get worn out easily, some experience pain, headaches, fatigue; this continues till their new body postures get used to the process. It is important to note that growing and getting optimal results as a yoga practitioner takes time and patience. It must be done with a gradual mastery of self, while cultivating stillness so as to facilitate chakra healing.

CRYSTALS

Crystals are super unique in nature. They play a major role in drawing out or redirecting energy in the chakras. Their purpose also involves helping to develop the strengths associated with a particular stone used for rebalancing and healing.

Purpose

Crystals can be used in lots of ways to address different problems. One notable happens whenever we work with crystals and stones; they play a major role in helping us connect with the natural earth energy, which, in turn, nourish our strengths and gifts. On the other hands, this experience heightens our awareness to see and declutter our lives of what no longer serves us. It also helps us to connect to our gifts, heal and restore our balance.

How It's Implemented

When it comes to working with crystals, there are various ways to go about it. One common way to do that is by lying down in a quiet and comfy space. As you do so, place crystals that are particular to the chakras, and begin to meditate gradually. The stones get as at work immediately by amplifying what is going on in your mind, which could be drawing energy from a particular chakra, connecting to your gifts, settling your thoughts or working towards a set goal. Another common way to work with crystals is by keeping a small with you. As you do so, its energy frequency will continually resonate with you throughout the day. This can be achieved by wearing it on your neck as a pendant, on your hand, as a bracelet or carrying it in your pocket. Nevertheless, another to work with the crystals is by holding it in your left hand as you meditate. This way, the healing vibrations of the crystals resonate in your body.

Why/How It Works

Earlier, we have clearly established that everything is energy, which has the capacity to vibrate in its own frequency. Even each crystal has its own purpose and vibration. When you choose each crystal to work out something for you, you are technically aligning yourself to be drawn to it, and its vibrations which will resonate within you. (It also has physical or health benefits, too.) For instance, making use of rose quartz not just helps the heart chakra; it greatly helps in the reduction of high blood pressure, too. It is entirely related.

Pros/Cons of Using This Method

Pros: Crystals are precious, valuable and pleasing to the eyes. They are easy to use, and can serve many purposes. Another thing is that, when you get to hold a crystal that is suitable for what you are working on, you will know. You will feel the pulse vibrating in your hand.

Cons: Working with crystals is not a walk in the park. It will definitely take time to master how to make use of each of them. Also, finding the exact crystal you need appears to be a difficult task, but this has largely improved, with the presence of internet.

ESSENTIAL OILS

The practice of essential oil therapy is not a modern day invention; it is actually traceable to ancient times, which involves the use of natural compounds and elements obtainable from plants for curing certain health problems, and for wellness purposes at large.

Purpose

The discovery of the healing benefits of plants has contributed immensely to the medicine and the health of mankind. By finding out these benefits, experts have found ways to include them in our diet, distilling their scent to be inhaled, and preparing medicines to be taken and topically applied on specific affected areas. While we are aware that essential oils have pleasant fragrances, it is important to know that each plant has its energetic resonance, and is beneficial to the energy body and physical body. Another unique function of essential oils is that it helps to relax our minds by shifting our thoughts from pressure to where we are able to breathe and feel at ease. It is equally useful during intense exercises as it can be used to massage tensed muscles and treat various kinds of pain.

How It's Implemented

It is already established that chakras are useful in helping chakras heal. So, in this venture, get an essential oil specific to a particular chakra and apply five to six drops of it on the chakra. This actually has the capacity to ground, open or heal it. Select a few essentials and mix them in an oil carrier then apply them on the chakras directly or with the use of a cotton ball. Also, it is important to note that it is note safe to apply the essential oils just like that. They should be diluted in the oil carrier, before application to avoid adverse effects, like skin irritation. The oil carrier is called as such because it contains the main essential that is needed to achieve our curative purposes. A notable carrier oil out there is known as jojoba; it can be found in a local health store. Lastly, you can practice meditation after applying the essential oils so as to enhance your experience.

Why/How It Works

Contrary to simply having a pleasant fragrance, essential oils are largely known for possessing powerful functions. Firstly, they are very effective in facilitating chakra healing in such a way that they bring the energetic of the oil to the chakra, and eventually help us to connect with it. Healing easily gains access to our internal being simply because it happens on a base, and bypasses our brain as such. Secondly, healing is created in our energy and physical bodies, when they access them, and connect them together in synergy.

Pros/Cons of Using This Method

Pros: One unique thing about essential oil therapy is the ease with which it brings its own healing. In other words, those interested in it experience little or no constrains in accessing it. The quality oils are easy to find; you can carry them along with you, and most importantly, there are diverse ways in which they can be used. They include, creating blends and elixirs, diffusing them in your room and work spaces, applying them on the body etc.

Cons:

Due its high tendency to irritate, it is not advisable for it to be topically applied on the body, without carrier oil. This will ensure a discreet experience on the part of the user. Also, it is important to note that essential oils are not highly advisable to be taken, because of their tendencies to inflame the digestive tract. One reason for this is because some of the oils out there are adulterated. Lastly, a good number of these essentials oils are highly powerful; so, it is advised that they are used in conjunction with other safe healing modalities that will effectively help you achieve chakra balance.

FOOD AND DIET

Food plays a unique role in our body. It does not only help in its development and sustenance; it equally serves as a great way to support the energy body as well. This is why we need to be intentional about what we eat; because, they go a long way to facilitate the healing of your chakras energetically.

Purpose

The purpose of food and diet in chakra healing is it helps in the build-up and sustenance of your energy and physical bodies. So, watch what you eat. Eating healthy and consistently making articulate food choices go a long way to making your body heal and promoting higher vibration of your chakras.

How It's Implemented

The body is known to function at its best, whenever it receives foods that support its systems. On the other hand, there are foods that can be inflammatory to the skin. For instance, when it comes to the skin, digestion and joint health, diary and gluten can be inflammatory to them; while sugar is inflammatory to various body parts and systems.

REIKI, ACUPUNCTURE,
AND THE CHAKRAS

There are a couple of modalities to bear in mind, while working with a professional to rebalance the chakras. In this venture, we will focus just on Reiki and acupuncture.

Reiki is basically an energy healing technique used by a practitioner to channel unlimited life force energy to a patient or client. The purpose of this system is to support their emotional, spiritual, mental, physical healing and evolution. The practitioner is known as Reiki practitioner; he acts as a conduit, thereby using gentle placement of hands to aid in the balance of the chakras. For the sake of productive outcomes, it is recommended that anyone interested in Reiki must undergo it with a certified Reiki practitioner.

Acupuncture is basically another traditional technique which makes use of precise needle placement to heal emotional, physical and metal symptoms. There is no official consensus about its feasibility. On the other hand, acupuncture moves chi and there are notably acupuncture points on the chakras. In this light, it is safe to say that acupuncture can be employed to address some chakra imbalances. Again, note that it should be only be undertaken with a licensed practitioner.

Sugar is basically not good for our bodies as it can pose a lot of problems when they are consumed in large quantities. However, the ideal thing to do is to technically cut down a large amount of processed foods from your diet, such as white flour, white sugar and other junks. You will notice positive changes in your, when you begin to consume clean foods. By clean foods, we mean healthy, less processed foods, which are organic, grown and harvested and locally sourced, and prepared with ingredients that are beneficial for your body's needs. Since your energy body is directly connected to your physical body, more attention should be given to the latter. This is because, as you invest in your physical body, your energy benefits also.

Why/How It Works

It is already established that an organically structured intake of healthy foods is highly beneficial to your physical and energy body health. So, it is important that you become informed about which foods that is suitable for your body systems; what works and what doesn't. This will equally help you kick-start and promote vital growth progress in the body such as gland health, mental functions, bone growth, cell growth, bone growth and muscle organ. When these are in place, they go a long way to benefit your benefit your energy body.

Pro/Cons of Using This Method

Pros: One good thing about food and diet is that you are open to many options and choices on how to go about supporting your energy and physical body, which when implemented are bound to give you tangible results.

Cons: The idea of eating healthy will always appear to be a walk in the park, until it is time to get it done. In the real sense of it, clean, organic foods can be very expensive when sough for, and would require a lot of patience, discipline and focus to stick to them. On the other, the processed fast foods tend to be cheaper, more tempting to consume, and promises no inconvenience.

Maintaining Balance
in Your Daily Life

As we gradually begin to give into the power of our chakras, it is very important that we see the need to maintain our positive energy in this venture. Why is this so? This is because as our personal healing progresses, we do not want any negativity to contaminate this novel reality. So, maintaining positive energy enables us to keep our space clear and protected from contradictory agents as we keep our vibrations on a higher frequency. This ultimately helps to maintain chakra balance.

Consistently cultivate mindfulness and practice gratitude:

Practicing gratitude helps us to focus on the present; but when choose to complain, it gives room for depression and get us stuck in the past. On the other hand, moments of anxiety teaches us to worry, and blinds us from seeing the good things that the future holds for us. The truth remains that worrying never solved a problem. This is where mindfulness comes in. It teaches us to stay in present and accept the realities that life brings our way, without feeling dejected, but receiving them with light-heartedness, energy and joy. Practicing gratitude makes our vibrations to increase.

Maintain your energy through movement:

This is very important for the overall healing of your chakras. You can devise means to go about this such as practicing yoga, meditation, qi gong and other activities. They have to be geared towards helping you maintain clarity of mind, body and spirit.

Bless yourself with sacred white sage:

The sacred white sage is a popular herb used by the Native Americans, which noted particularly notable for its clearing properties, whenever it is applied. Back then, it was widely used to clear or sanitize the body of living spaces of negative energy. The very act of clearing our bodies or spaces with the sacred white sage is known as smudging. If you want to smudge your living space, the first thing to do is to get a bunch of a sage, and light up the tip with a match or lighter. Let the smoke settle for a while, before you use your hand to waft it to various areas of your apartment. Let the movement be clockwise direction, and then you might want to start from the front door to items in the room then back to the door, saying words of blessings. If you want to smudge yourself, direct the movement of the smoke to yourself, saying words of blessings to your body parts, and do not forget your chakras. Ensure that you tap the loose ashes in a plate to avoid messing up the place. As you go on, let your words be lie, "I bless my heart chakra, my chest, my arms…" and so on.

Epsom salt baths

Epsom salt baths contains Magnesium which is very helpful in detoxifying the system against cold, aches and pain. When applied on the skin, it absorbs the pain effects, leaving a soothing and ameliorating impact. It is highly recommended for sensitive people. Also, Epsom salt baths help to clear auras, making it good for people working in toxic offices, work long hours or under duress.

Your Sacred Healing Space

A healing space is basically the centre point, where you specially chose to stay and nurture your healing.

To make this happen, here are recommended items that you must keep in mind:

Sacred white sage bundle: it is already established that the purposed of a sacred white sage is for smudging yourself and a space. The directive remains the same. If you want to smudge a place, light up the tip of cloth, let the smoke settle a bit, before wafting it round the place to be smudged.

Palo Santo: Pablo Santo embodies similar unique features with sacred white sage. It actually sanitizes the atmosphere of negative energy and tension, especially evil spirits. Pablo Santo is also known as "holy wood" in Spanish, and originally comes from a tree that is grown in Central and South America.

Feather Wand: It is used to regulate the direction of the smoke used in smudging. Some have a single feather, while others can be full of weathers.

Heat-resistant container: Make use of this to gather the ashes that will eventually fall from the Pablo Santo or white sage.

Crystal allies: It is important that you keep some crystals aside. You will need it to occasionally bless the alter space and, of course, to raise the vibration of your alter.

Photos of ancestors and loved ones: One powerful thing about our existence here is that it the energy of our being cum essence does not diminish, when we pass away. Our impacts still remain in the hearts of those who hold us dear. So, as you set up your altar, keep photos of your loved ones, who have passed on. It strongly honours their memories and evokes their energy, protection, presence and wisdom.

Candles: Lighting candles is a very key item in your routines in the altar's space. It serves as an avenue to invoke the alter energy, honour your ancestors and connect to the Divine.

Symbolic statues of deities: This is another key item for an ideal altar. Some people prefer to keep the statues of deities that they have a close relationship with, to enable connect better with them.

An offering bowl: This is usually a bowl or container for putting offerings of fruits, money, water or flowers.

Nevertheless, it is needful to maintain a clean environment for the sustenance of peace and positive energy in the atmosphere. Have an efficient system that allows for regular cleanings. Ensure that dirt and unnecessary materials are decluttered from the room; because, having them stagnant makes ways for negative energy to abide.

Place crystals beside your gadgets at home, offices or work spaces. This is because it helps to create balance in the atmosphere. Black tourmaline is known for its quality absorbing and blocking capacities on electromagnetic pollutions emitted by the devices.

More so, a good way to protect ourselves from harm or the toxicity of the workplace is by setting up a crystal grid. This goes a long way to help stabilize atmosphere from possible pollutions that might arise occasionally. How do you go about this? Take four crystals and put them in the four corners of the room such as black tourmaline, clear quartz, selenite etc. This is not only applicable to office; it can also be done in your homes (bed frame, curtain, corners of the room.)

Unlike we have done previously, the next section will us have going into details about the exact state of our mental, spiritual, physical, and emotional health, when our chakras are not balanced. We will cover the ailments and the symptoms, and of course, study the healing techniques involved accordingly.

II

HEALING YOUR CHAKRAS

In part 2, you will be putting your new knowledge to use by making use of self-healing techniques to address common ailments. Chapter 3 is basically an overview of about forty sicknesses and symptoms that are associated with imbalanced chakras. Chapter 4 opens you up to a wide range of healing techniques that can be used to heal and restore balance your chakra system.

3

■■□□□ ■■

COMMON SYMPTOMS
AND AILMENTS

We are naturally inclined to know when something does not sit right in our being. We get the signals not just in the physical sense of it; but, there are also manifest emotional, spiritual and mental symptoms. In this chapter, we will be basically looking at various common ailments and symptoms that are largely experienced, when the chakras are not balanced. We will look at them in alphabetical order as well as the charkas which are affected. These symptoms can range from simple ones, like fatigue, neck pain, headache to even complicated issues like cancer, depression and addiction. Because different symptoms exist for different ailments, there will be a handful of explanations in that regard.

Addiction

CHAKRAS AFFECTED   *although other chakras are involved; the throat chakra is mostly affected.*

Addiction is the outcome we have, when we overly depend on a legal or illegal drug, substance, food or habit(s) for happiness or ease. It poses a lot of risks to a lot of important things we hold dear, including our relationships, and of course, our spiritual, mental, physical health, and our work. When we are deeply addicted, we tend to be disconnected with ourselves and others, making us unable to properly express our feelings. These signs indicate that the throat chakra is imbalanced.

Despite the fact that addiction is majorly related to the throat chakra, it has been observed that other chakras can propel the addition to continue existing. When we begin to feel less appreciated or ashamed of whom we are, or take pain-numbing substances, our sacral plexus chakra is involved in the picture. Feelings of low self-esteem or powerlessness indicate that our solar sacral plexus chakra is affected. If we feel that our addiction is our only source of ease and balance, then our root chakra may be at huge risk. If we do it to heal our anxieties or broken hearts, then our heart chakra is actively involved. When we feel alone and deeply disconnected from the Divine, it indicates that our root chakra is involved.

Lastly, it is interesting to know that addictions can vary. And, one of them could be something as simple as the ability to perceive, understand or trust things which are beyond the natural (psychic abilities). The addictive behaviour could be to enhance this ability or numb it simply because it is weird to the person.

Adrenal Fatigue

CHAKRAS AFFECTED   *root chakra, sacral plexus chakra*

Adrenal fatigue is simply the outcome we have, when we are exposed to chronic stress. This is how it works. When we constantly undergo heavy stress, our adrenal glands tend to become exhausted, therefore, subjecting the adrenal health to an insufficient state. This is basically a state, where it is incapable of producing hormones for the balance and proper functioning of the body. Specifically, the adrenal glands naturally release cortisol, the stress hormone, which handles stress. On the other hand, adrenaline is also released. We are better off, when both are in place as we navigate stressful situations. However, when undergo stress continually; we put our adrenal glands at risk from keeping us going. This is to say that victims of adrenal fatigue have been on the run, without checking themselves. That is not nice!

Nevertheless, let's look at some signs of adrenal fatigue. They include loss of body hair, headache, general tiredness, body aches, low blood pressure, skin discolouration (hyper pigmentation), and weight loss. There is a need to explore the root chakra and the sacral plexus chakra since they are the chakras of the adrenal glands, which are associated with stress. The sacral plexus chakra is related to issues surrounding power and self-esteem; while the root chakra deals with issues related to feeling grounded, stable and secured.

Anger

CHAKRAS AFFECTED   *although other chakras are involved; the root chakra is mostly affected.*

Anger is not entirely a negative emotion. It can also be described as a positive or healthy emotion. It actually helps us to set boundaries against what is wrong, stand up for ourselves, escape harm and protect ourselves. Anger only tends to be highly destructive to ourselves and others, when expressed in the wrong way or channelled in the wrong direction.

In most situations, anger is induced by fear. This fear boils down to fear of the future, of the unknown, of our livelihood, of our safety etc. As a result, anger is deeply related to the root chakra; it is also our survival chakra.

Whenever our anger is induced by fear, it seriously affects the balance of other chakras. There are signs that indicate the imbalance of such. For instance, our crown chakra is eventually distorted, when we are angry towards the Divine/God/Universe for making life so unfair or unjust to us. Also, our third eye chakra is also affected, when we gradually begin to lose touch with our emotional intelligence and only focus on our intellect. Our throat chakra is equally affected, when we are angry and unable to express our feelings. If we are heartbroken to the point of feeling lonely, stressed and harbouring unforgiveness, then our heart chakra needs healing and balance. If our anger comes from a place of being displaced or feeling out of control of our lives, then our solar plexus chakra needs to be balanced.

Lastly, if our anger affects our creativity and affects our ability to express ourselves, then our sacral plexus chakra is out of balance and needs healing. However, there are times, when our anger turns out to be brimming and even explode in the process. Also, it is important to know that sexual abuse can crumple our emotions, making us easily temperamental.

Anorexia and Bulimia

CHAKRAS AFFECTED   *solar plexus chakra*

Anorexia is basically an eating disorder that stems from having a distorted view of oneself, and fear of gaining weight. People suffering from anorexia tend to follow strict eating routines, and often end up eating so little. However, Bulimia is basically when someone has an uncontrolled overfeeding eating lifestyle; this includes binging on junks and real foods, and eventually ends up vomiting or purging. Both eating disorders are so extreme, and both result from a flawed perception of oneself and appearance, which is unhealthy. For instance, this is what we have when people equate their worth to their weight or body size. So, they adopt unhealthy dieting routines to alter their body size to suit their taste. The presence of anorexia and bulimia, in an individual, result to an imbalance of the solar plexus chakra. It is basically responsible for issues around control, power and confidence.

Anxiety

We all occasionally suffer anxiety as we walk through life. However, it can be frustrating when it becomes consistent and intense. This type of anxiety can morph into fear or intense worry within minutes, and equally come in –between the qualities of our lives.

It is already established that every type of anxiety we have is associated or involved with a particular type of chakra. For example, if we begin to feel we have a distorted relationship with the Divine or universe, it simply indicates that our crown chakra is out of balance. If we begin to feel unnecessarily tensed up and uncertain about the unknown, it is a sign that our third eye chakra is out of balance. Our anxiety is prompted by our throat chakra, if we become anxious about expressing our minds, sharing our thoughts and communicating with others. If we are heartbroken, malicious, and unforgiving, it could be that our heart chakra is imbalanced. If we begin to feel intimidated, overwhelmed by life, and feeling the pressure to perform to impress, then our anxiety is caused by our imbalanced solar plexus chakra. Feelings of shamed or guilt is basically prompted, when our root chakra is out of balance. This also occurs, when we have a history of trauma, whether healed or not. It also comes with the anxiety of our basic human needs such as food, shelter and money.

Asthma and Allergies

CHAKRAS AFFECTED   *heart chakra*

The existence of narrow airways in our bodies has the tendency to trigger coughing, wheezing and shortness of breath; especially when they produce mucus. The presence of allergies causes our immune system to mark each allergen, even if the case might be different. Either ways, they have the possibility of affecting the quality of our lives. Sometimes, conditions, like these, stem from a weak immune system, which, in turn, may result to symptoms such as breathing problems, inflammation in our skin, airways, sinuses or digestive system. The bottom line is that these physical symptoms are manifest because they are related to the heart. And, they are directly related to an imbalance in the heart chakra, especially, if we are having problems about love, compassion, grief and heartache.

Back Pain

Back pain is basically any common, but painful occurrence on any area of the back–upper back, middle back or lower back–which is mostly caused by trauma, stress or an underlying disease. However, it has been discovered that the presence of back pain reflects the state of our chakra health. On the other hand, symptoms of back pain range from burning sensation, headache, fatigue and acute muscle tightening which can worsen when you bend, stand or walk.

UPPER BACK

CHAKRAS AFFECTED *heart chakra, throat chakra*

It is amazing to know how various types of back pain indicate something about the state of our chakra. For instance, when we are having heartbreaks, difficulties in loving ourselves and others, this underlying experience has a way of physically showing itself as pain in the upper back area. This pain also manifests when we hold back love or feeling unloved, unsupported.

MIDDLE BACK

CHAKRAS AFFECTED   *heart chakra, solar plexus chakra*

The experience is different in this case as it is majorly related to matters of love. When we experience difficulties in loving, unforgiving or feeling unsettled in our power, the tension physically manifests itself as tension or pain in the middle area of the back. On the hand, this feeling can be prompted, when we are held back by past hurts or awash with a sense of guilt about our mistakes.

LOWER BACK

CHAKRAS AFFECTED   *sacral plexus chakra, root chakra*

In this case, feeling challenged in certain areas has a way of prompting tension or pain in our lower back area. These areas include our abundance, relationships, creative expression etc. For instance, when we neither hold back emotions nor refuse to process them; this is also seen when we are having issues around survival as we go about catering for our needs. Most interestingly, we also tend to have back pain not necessarily through trauma; but, when we feel financially unsupported.

Cancer

Cancer is a deadly disease which it occurs as a result of the development of abnormal cells, which, in turn, spread uncontrollably to infiltrate and destroy the normal body tissues. It can occur on various parts of a human body, and its symptoms vary according to the place of its occurrence. Some of these symptoms include fatigue, skin changes, weight loss, inexplicable joint or muscle pain, inexplicable persistent fevers or night sweats, lumps or thickening areas under the skin. There are factors that are known to increase the risk of cancer such as habits, family history, health conditions, age and environment.

On the other hand, it has been observed that a lot of cancer victims do not posses any risk factor(s) at all. As it regards energy, when we harbour perpetual resentment and deep hurt in our hearts, without processing or attending to it, the result of it can be cancer. They bear fruits in forms of anger, grief, hatred or other toxic emotions that eats the soul away.

These are various levels in which these manifest as a result of imbalance in certain chakras:

- Breast cancer: Heart chakra

- Cancers of stomach, liver, intestines and pancreas: solar plexus chakra
- Brain tumours: Crown chakra
- Prostate and rectal cancer: Sacral plexus and root chakras
- Lung cancer: Throat and heart chakras

Codependency

CHAKRAS AFFECTED   *heart chakra, solar plexus chakra, sacral plexus chakra, root chakra*

Being in a failing, one-sided relationship, where we majorly rely on our partners for our emotional and spiritual needs; we are said codependent. In other words, codependency is basically a type of relationship, where a partner's flaws or irresponsibility prompts his significant other to sacrifice his or her needs to care for and help the said partner to the point of giving up a major part of themselves, including accruing, low self-esteem, poor mental health, and financial and emotional instability. It is important to note that a major reason for the existence of codependent relationships is based on fear and rejection, which has a direct link to an imbalance in the root chakra. Fear-based actions and feelings are tied to the root chakra.

Codependency often has its foundation from childhood, when a dysfunctional home refuses to acknowledge the presence of pain, fear, anger or shame. This can be seen when a family is hooked in addiction or the presence of sexual, verbal or physical; or, if one is suffering from any mental or physical sickness. It is also notable that issues of ignored family issues are related to the root chakra.

More so, the existence of codependency indicates of the imbalance of the heart chakra simply because it is related to the matters of the heart. And, in this case, we tend to focus on loving and caring for others instead of doing the same to ourselves. This disconnection is unhealthy for us, because we can only have true happiness when we place value and love on ourselves. Imbalance of the heart chakra can result to lack of discernment in relationships.

Lastly, the damage done to our self-esteem indicates that the stability of our solar chakra plexus is affected. Then when we begin to have feelings relating to lack of healthy boundaries, shame, guilt, anger and resentment in our codependent relationships, it indicates that the stability of our sacral plexus chakra is affected.

Conflict

Conflict is simply a state of disagreement between two or more parties over a certain matter or issues. They can never have a head way as long as the individuals involved continue to disagree. Understanding or consent is needful for progress to be made in that venture. Whenever we have a problem with communicating or basically expressing ourselves, the throat chakra is involved. Sometimes, one way we commonly use to avoid conflict is by staying silent. Keeping quiet over certain sensitive issues makes us resentful and it gives room for those unvoiced feelings in our hearts to pile up, until we eventually get to explode. We are naturally wired to express ourselves and communicate how we feel. So, whether we seek conflict or try to avoid it, our throat chakra is striving to be heard.

On the other hand, the presence of conflict could be a sign of imbalance in our solar plexus chakra, which is related to issues concerning power. It could also indicate that our sacral plexus chakra needs attention since it is the seat of our emotions.

Constipation

<u>CHAKRAS AFFECTED</u>   *root chakra, possibly solar plexus chakra*

Constipation is simply the inability to pass bowels frequently as a normal human being should. The causes are mainly to changes in diet routines or intake of diets that lack sufficient fibre. When we experience constipation, it could be an indication that our root chakra is out of balance; this is chiefly because the rectum and anus are at the level of the root chakra. Interestingly, constipation is basically traced to an imbalance in the digestive system. It is also important to know that the state of the solar plexus chakra determines the state of the digestive system. Other factors that affect the digestive system are experiences include tension, fear, lack of confidence and self-respect, and feeling out of touch with our power. They go ahead to create certain disorders such as colon, intestinal problems etc.

Depression

CHAKRAS AFFECTED   *heart chakra, crown chakras*

There are many reasons we undergo depression. While it can be temporarily present for a while, other times, it is appears to be stagnant. Most times, constant depression can be achingly frustrating. Its symptoms range from sadness, emptiness, memory loss, loneliness, despair, absence of happiness or pleasure in our day-to-day activities. Depression runs deeper than it appears than it appears to, and poses greater risks to our existence and overall well being. To be specific, it affects our sleep, focus and eventually propels us to commit suicide by replaying scary such thoughts in our minds.

A major cause of depression is loneliness. We are social beings; we were wired to interact with other people in order to make the best of our existence. So, being in lonely situations, over time, weighs down the soul and eventually has a way of triggering feelings of depression. However, it is important to note that depression is linked to the crown chakra. It is balanced when we are in touch with the universe and the Divine. This leaves us focused, at ease and with a peaceful feeling. On the other hand, the presence of depression is an indicator that our crown chakra is no longer in harmony. It equally means that we are disconnected from our world, and angry with Divinity at the present state of things in our lives. Also, depression can also come when our heart chakra is not in harmony.

Digestive Issues

CHAKRA AFFECTED   *solar plexus chakra*

Digestive issues are often prompted by the changes in our diet routines. It can be debilitating in such a way that puts us very uncomfortable. If it begins to affect us physically, then we will also feel it in our energy. This ailment is strongly linked to our solar plexus chakra, which is also related to our power centre. When this chakra is out of harmony, we are left with feeling powerless, intimidated, having low self-esteem etc. The presence of these negative feelings can lead to the rise of digestive issues in our systems.

Disconnected from self and others

Feelings associated with being disconnected from ourselves and people are normal occurrences that we experience occasionally. However, when it is constant, it clearly indicates that our heart chakra is out of balance. One symptom of it is frustration. However, we eventually tend to get back in touch with ourselves once more; but, in a way that lightens up our heart and spirits. We are still bereft of that sure sense of knowing. Other feelings associated with this include despair, not contented with life, absence of pleasure or happiness. We find ourselves in places or situations that arouse our joy, but do not feel it at all. Also, a perpetual disconnection from others can further lead depression.

Interestingly, a lot of people who are disconnected from themselves or people do not know. Instead, they are too busy or buried in their schedules to know. We only know that we are connected to ourselves and others, when we operate from a place of awareness and gratitude. Doing this not only helps us to create deeper connection with ourselves, but with a more healthy connection with our heart chakra.

Fatigue

CHAKRAS AFFECTED   *solar plexus chakra, crown chakra*

Fatigue is basically a constant feeling of weariness and unwillingness to work caused by exhaustion. This out rightly affects our peace of mind, focus, sleep, energy and motivation. We are left without energy to work, because it has been heavily depleted. Some types of activities or habits are known to easily make us prone to having fatigue such as habitual busyness, overworking ourselves etc.

Interestingly, fatigue is directly linked to our solar plexus chakra, which is also our power centre. So, it can be risky to tie our self-esteem and self-confidence to our performances in the work place. This is because when we fail to perform very well, we will be under pressure to outdo ourselves in subsequent times, finally leading to fatigue. On the other hand, when we are fatigued due to depression or disconnected from the Divine, then it is a sign that our crown chakra is our harmony.

Fear

CHAKRAS AFFECTED   *solar plexus chakra, root chakra*

Fear is a feeling that is prompted by perceptions of an impending danger or something harmful to our existence is coming our way. When we are afraid, the brain quickly alters the state of our organs in such a way that activates our nervous system and puts us into flight or fight mode. As a matter of fact, fear plays a key role in our survival here in the universe. The presence of fear helps us to identify threats, natural disasters and survive them. However, the negative impact of fear in our lives begins, when it has stayed for so long. Always worrying about how to survive our daily challenges and overcome threats in our families and communities serve as triggers to this kind of fear.

The stability of our basic needs such as clothing, feeding and shelter are important and influence the impact of fear in our lives. When they are threatened, our root chakra subsequently goes out of harmony. If we are not educated on how to overcome this fear, early enough in life, it will result to more damages to our hormones, leading to adrenal fatigue.

On the other hand, apart from our root chakra, our solar plexus chakra is equally affected whenever we feel fear. Since they both have a link to power, being grounded and self-esteem, threats to the stability or availability of our basic needs has a way of making us feel powerless and less of ourselves.

Grief

heart chakra

Misfortunes come to us, once in a while, such as losing a property or a loved one. And, when it does, it is healthy to grieve. However, if we ignore the existence of grief over time or hold onto hurting memories, it can cause our heart chakra to go out of harmony. This imbalance further result to feelings of loneliness, despair and even make us cultivate bitterness. There is a high tendency to withdraw from others while grieving. It is healthy sometimes, because it helps us to better process what we are going through and how we feel.

However, since our heart chakra has a link to self-love and our love for others, staying away for a long time makes our heart chakra to suffer due to lack of connection. While grieving, it is important that we acknowledge the need to be in touch with ourselves and others so as to ensure that our heart chakra stays in harmony.

Guilt

CHAKRA AFFECTED   *solar plexus chakra, sacral plexus chakra*

Guilt is basically a feeling that stems from having done something wrong. However, this emotion has a strong relation to our sacral plexus chakra, which is basically known as the seat of our emotions; it is also associated with the emotions of our sexuality and pleasure. Our awareness or enlightenment on matters related to our emotions influences how we overcome them. If we are taught to repress our emotions as kids, we would easily feel guilty and shame as adults.

On the other hand, guilt has a positive impact in our lives; but, interestingly, it is a negative emotion that impedes us from enjoying happiness and pleasure. The presence of these emotions is indicates that our sacral plexus chakra is in harmony. When guilt affects our self-esteem and sense of power, it is a sign that our solar plexus chakra is out balance. Lastly, a key remedy to feelings of guilt, other than the aforementioned ones, is simply allowing ourselves to process our feelings instead of repressing them.

Headache

<u>CHAKRAS AFFECTED</u>   *third eye chakra, crown chakra*

Headaches are commonly felt, when we are stressed or sick; but, when they do not come as a result of nay physical illness, then it can be traced to an imbalance in one of our chakras. Frontal headaches that manifests symptoms of sinus pressure and pressure behind your eyes that can spread to your forehead, it can be traced to an imbalance in the third eye chakra. This type of headache is unique, and suggests that we are majorly focusing on our intellect, while neglecting the realities and possibilities of the spiritual. More so, it means that we are just being rational, only seeing things as they are. Other researches affirm that the presence of this headache signals how much we ignore the inner wisdom we possess, and the need to embrace it for good. For instance, if you have a premonition about an impending occurrence or about to pursue a course, but refuse to follow your intuition, and choose to go merely go after it, such can cause your third eye chakra to be in disharmony.

On the other hand, the presence of a vertex headache indicates the imbalance of the root chakra. A vertex headache actually occurs at the top centre of the head. The presence of this type of headache suggests our reluctance or failure to trust our life's path or journey, seeing the bigger shape of things, cultivating trust in ourselves and neglecting our connection to the Divine. It also has the tendency to induce feelings of loneliness and dissatisfaction in us.

Hermorrhoids

CHAKRA AFFECTED   *root chakra*

Hemorrhoids are also known as piles. They are swollen veins and lower rectum, which are located in two places. The one located under the skin, around the anus, is called *external hemorrhoids*, while the one inside the rectum is known as *internal hemorrhoids*. Their causes range from straining while passing bowels to strain caused by pregnancy or even by a chakra imbalance.

Since the rectum and anus are at the same level with the root chakra, the presence of this dysfunction or ailment indicates that the root chakra is out of balance. This chakra is majorly about our survival, so, there may be huge quest to meet our basic needs such as shelter, feeding, clothing and staying at peace. On the part of energy, hemorrhoids can be prompted by feeling burdened, holding onto past hurts and fear of letting go.

Hip Pain

CHAKRA AFFECTED   *sacral plexus chakra*

Issues associated with pains, tension, tightness and muscle spasms in the hips are either caused by trauma or over exercising. However, these defects can be traced to issues related to sacral plexus chakra. Interestingly, the hips have a way of harbouring lots of emotions, especially we have been ignoring or yet to be processed. Since the sacral plexus chakra is the seat of our emotions, ignoring our emotions over time can result to an imbalance in the chakra. More so, if we are having trouble with expressing our sexuality in a healthy manner, especially as regards confidence or shame, such can result to pain or tightness in the hips.

Infertility

CHAKRA AFFECTED   *root chakra, sacral plexus chakra, solar plexus chakra*

Infertility is simply defined as a situation where a woman is unable to conceive despite a couple of attempts for at least a year or two. Infertility is commonly experienced by lots of women; but then, the stress and frustration encountered by such women often leaves them with feelings of fear, distress and even shame. Once more, the sacral plexus chakra is involved here not just because it is located round the womb and genitals; but, because it is the seat of emotions.

You may not be able to imagine what women battling with infertility go through from day to day. It ranges from emotional distress, loss of appetite, weight loss due to constant worry etc. Some often wonder: "Is this the right place for me?" "Can I be able to conceive?" "Am I married to the right person?" "How will I cope after now?"

Sometimes, infertility can stem from certain physical causes such as lack of menstruation, poor egg quality, low sperm count, high follicle-stimulating hormone (FSH) etc. However, it could be that such persons, in question, constantly undergo extreme stressful activities that are unhealthy for their condition. When infertility begins to trigger issues in the family, the root chakra comes into the equation. One of them could be a sense of dissatisfaction from the other family members as a result of this condition. Instead of being compassionate, they feel that the lady will pass on such trait to their family. Also, when the pressures of infertility begin to make the individuals involved powerless or hurt their self-esteem, it can result to an imbalance in the solar plexus chakra.

Jaw Pain/Temporomandibular Joint (TMJ) Pain

CHAKRA AFFECTED   *throat chakra*

The jaw bone is connected to your skull by the Temporomandibular Joint (TMJ). It also acts as a sliding lever that allows it to open and close, with one joint at each side of one jaw. Sometimes, there could be pain in areas of the joint, with causes ranging from arthritis, jaw injury, genetics, teeth grinding, teeth clenching and grinding or bruxism. Interestingly, pain in the joint can also manifest, when we feel silenced or when we continually hold back what we want to say. For the sake of therapy, wearing a mouth guard at night can be helpful to ameliorate jaw pain.

However, as we move on, it is important to note that TMJ pain runs deep, and could be also be rooted in our energies; that is, when we feel silenced, unable to communicate effectively or say what we actually mean. We can also experience TMJ pain, when we are feeling hurt or angry. So, as we find solutions to the physical pains, addressing the energetic causes will go a long way to help, too. BE intentional about communicating effectively, and whenever you feel held back from expressing your thoughts, take a pause and examine what it really is, and why it is difficult to do so.

Leg Pain

CHAKRA AFFECTED   *root chakra, solar plexus chakra*

Leg pain is basically a pain in any part of the leg that often caused by trauma. If it's not traceable to trauma, then such is caused by an imbalance of the root chakra. This type of pain is known to manifest, when we hold back from making progress in life especially due to fear of failure or of what negative thing might happen to us. This imbalance of the root chakra can be directly linked to the solar plexus chakra; but, it mainly revolves around the root chakra since such fears are associated with our basic needs for survival such as clothing, feeding and shelter.

Loneliness

CHAKRA AFFECTED   *heart chakra*

Loneliness is a powerful feeling that we experience once in a while especially in our down times. Such feeling translates to the fact that we are not connected to anyone. However, our heart chakra constantly reminds us that were hard wired to not just socialise with others, but also to love and connect with them. Love is the biggest experience we need to keep our heart chakra balanced. The moment we lose touch with others is the moment we begin to lose touch with ourselves and our heart chakra, resulting to loneliness.

What could cause such feeling of loneliness is holding onto past hurts and pain. The fact remains that it is difficult to heal from such, when we have refused to let go. Such shuts our hearts from connecting with others, and no matter how much we try to do, our hearts will still be heavy and not radiate with joy. Release begins with letting go of the past, loving ourselves and others. This enables us to connect with our heart chakra and withers any feeling of loneliness in us.

Neck Pain

CHAKRA AFFECTED   *throat chakra*

If neck pain is not induced by any trauma of any kind, then it can be traceable to an imbalance of the throat chakra. This occurs when we refuse to communicate our thoughts effectively in the world or when we hold back from speaking our truths sincerely and openly as a result of fear or insecurity of any kind. For instance, these experiences play out in toxic relationships, where we pretend to be happy, when all is not well. Another instance could be in work spaces, where are scared to speak out for fear of what people will say or think of us. Other reasons abide for why we occasionally do not share our thoughts or express ourselves sincerely. The consequences remain an imbalance in our throat chakra that manifests as pain in the neck region.

Neuropathy

CHAKRA AFFECTED   *third eye chakra*

Neuropathy is basically an ailment which manifests itself through pain at a particular part or throughout the body. Neuropathy is mostly caused by damage to the nerves, and others which include uncontrolled diabetes, traumatic injury, side effects of chemotherapy, hereditary factors etc. However, if the cause is not traceable to these aforementioned names, then it is the result of an imbalance of the third eye chakra, since it has a direct link to neurological issues.

A notable sign of imbalance in this chakra is when being disconnected from our intuition; in other words, when hold back from connecting to the spiritual dimensions of our existence, the result is pain throughout the body. Sometimes, the fear arises simply because we are on the verge of connecting to our spiritual selves, and are uncertain of our power or what will become of us.

Panic Attacks

CHAKRAS AFFECTED   *heart chakra, solar plexus chakra, root chakra*

It is really easy to have panic attacks, when we are caught up in tensed situations that grip us with sudden, acute and disabling anxiety. Some symptoms of panic attacks include pounding heart, fear, trembling, sweat, palpitations, shaking, increased heart rate, shortness of breath and a sense of an oncoming danger. On the other hand, these signs strongly indicate that we are disconnected from our heart chakra. It is also a sign that we are ignoring the heeding and promptings of our heart. An important thing to note about the chakras is their ability to react, when we refuse to comply with them.

More so, panic attacks are related to our root chakra, because that is where our sense of power lies. We begin to powerless and the need to survive. The disconnection of our heart chakra also affects solar plexus chakra, which controls our self-esteem and sense of confidence.

Sciatica

Sciatica is basically a painful condition in which pain originating from the spine runs down to the legs, lower back, abdomen and buttocks. It is often caused by trauma on the herniated disc or bone in the spine causing it to press on the nerve. On the hand, another cause of this can be traced to an imbalance in the root chakra. It has been already established that the root chakra controls issues surrounding our survival and sense of being. When we are afflicted with sciatic pain, we become worried about how to carter for our basic needs such as feeding, clothing and shelter. We live in fear that we may not be able to achieve these things.

Nevertheless, the presence of sciatica could be an indication that we are living under the fear of money. When we begin to feel pain that prevents us from walking comfortably, it is important that we find out whether we are scared to make progress in life or go to the places where our destinies can be fulfilled. Sciatica can also be linked to a feeling of insecurity in the world. It could also mean that we are repressing our creative prowess, ignoring our emotions or denying ourselves from enjoying the abiding pleasures of life.

Self-Hate

CHAKRAS AFFECTED   *heart chakra, solar plexus chakra, root chakra*

Self-hate is basically the opposite of self-love. It is the agonistic feeling that stems from the perception that we are not loved or unlovable due to one reason or the other. This feeling also originates from how people are treated, when they are kids. A lot of people, who grow up under verbal or physical abuse, most likely end up battling their self-esteem; they find it difficult to give or receive love from others. On the other hand, the existence of this issue indicates an imbalance in our heart chakra. When we are disconnected from our heart chakra, we gradually cease to have love and compassion towards ourselves and others.

Nevertheless, nursing hatred towards ourselves is not entirely ordinary. On many occasions, it stems from anger, which is notably a sensitive and strong emotion. And, anger has its roots in fear. We suddenly become scared of our existence and the inability to carter for our means of survival. When these issues begin to mature, it is a sign that root chakra is out of harmony. This is because it is related to our centre of power and survival. If this fear begins to affect our self-esteem, then it is a sign that our solar plexus chakra is affected.

On self-hate, it is one thing to perceive that we are unlovable; but, it is another thing to know that this knowledge can be changed. In essence, as we begin to reconnect back to our heart chakra, we renew our love and compassion towards others, and most importantly to ourselves.

Sexual Abuse

CHAKRAS AFFECTED   *throat chakra, solar plexus chakra, root chakra, sacral plexus chakra*

Sexual abuse is an experience nobody would wish to have. The scary aspect of it is that it does not only damage our physical bodies, it threatens the peace of our souls. The traumas run so deep, causing the victims to alienate themselves from their feelings, people and even their immediate environment so as to avoid getting more hurt. Subsequently, they feel shame and blame themselves for being available for such experience. Their emotions may become unstable, making them often temperamental in unlikely situations. In most cases, this anger is targeted not just to themselves; but, to their abusers, who are the primary cause of such trauma. This also leads to making feel dislodged and powerless. These reactions are said to be related to the sacral plexus chakra.

However, in cases where the abuse was perpetrated by a family member, after which other family refuses to support the victim or agitate for justice, the victim would eventually feel betrayed. This feeling is related to the root chakra. Also, if the feeling remains ignored and unprocessed for a while, thereby affecting the self-esteem or self-confidence of the victim, then the solar plexus chakra is affected. As a result of the trauma, the victim might feel silenced or scared to share his or her experience on the matter. This indicates that the throat chakra is affected.

It is important to note that exercising our throat chakra is a safe route towards emotional healing. This is because what silence does is to keep us comfortable in pain; but, opening up our hearts and sharing our burden will put us at ease eventually. While doing this could be scary, it is advisable to speak to counsellor or emotional healing expert.

Shame

<u>CHAKRAS AFFECTED</u> *sacral plexus chakra, solar plexus chakra*

Shame is simply a feeling that makes see ourselves as undesirable and lesser than who we are. It is how we feel after we have been humiliated for a misdemeanour or depraving from the morally accepted way of doing things. Our imperfections are mainly what makes us feel shame; especially, when they are not appreciated or acknowledged by those around us. Such feelings strongly affect our sacral plexus chakra because it is the seat of our emotions. This is also where our sexual passions are nurtured. Prolonged feelings of shame can dislodge our self-worth and eventually put us as risk of losing our confidence. When this begins to occur, it indicates that our solar plexus chakra is out of harmony.

Sinus Pain

CHAKRA AFFECTED   *third eye chakra*

Sinus pain stems from the inflammation of the sinus. The symptoms range from the pain around the nose, eyes, neck and chest regions. It is an allergic reaction; but, if this pain is not related as such, then it indicates a disharmony in the third eye chakra. This chakra is mainly concerned about our ability to see beyond the realities of this realm. It helps us to perceive information beyond what we can see with our physical eyes, and be insightful.

Other causes of sinus pain could be traced to the fact that we are either irritated or uncomfortable with a person that, making us to feel alienated from such person. In cases, like this, it is important that we examine the reason for this to avoid making conclusions with assumptions that are not true.

Sexually Transmitted Infections (STIs)

Sexually infected diseases and infections are basically contracted during sexual intercourse with an already infected person. If the cause does not stem from here, then it indicates that there may be an imbalance in the sacral plexus chakra. Interestingly, this chakra is related to and deals with our sexuality and sexual perceptions including the emotional aspects, relationships and other issues therein.

However, our feelings and sexual perceptions play a major role on STIs reoccur in our lives. For instance, shame is a notable one. When we begin to shameful after a sexual experience overtime, we contract STIs. This calls our attention to how much we need to re-evaluate and debunk lots of myths about our sexual perceptions and feelings, because oftentimes they appear to be wrong or even outdated. Doing this would eventually impact our healing in the long-run. Our sacral plexus chakra can only be healed, when the toxic views of our sexuality are healed.

Skin Issues

__CHAKRA AFFECTED__   *crown chakra*

The skin is the largest organ in the body. It is also about the most unique. However, hormonal issues, environmental changes and complications in diet regimen can cause many disorders such as rashes, rosacea, acne, eczema, dermatitis etc. When these skin disorders do not stem from any of the aforementioned reasons, it indicates that our crown chakra is out harmony. If it is true, then there is an urgent need to examine our lives to see where we have disconnected from the Divine and even our spirituality. Lacking faith in the former can result to such disorders. This tells us that being at peace with the Divine makes our skin glow; and, keeps our crown chakra in harmony.

Stomach Pain and Disorders

__CHAKRA AFFECTED__   *solar plexus chakra*

Causes of stomach pain and disorders include ulcer, diarrhoea, constipation, indigestion, gastritis, acid reflux, inflammatory bowel syndrome (IBS), colon/intestinal problems etc. Having a complicated diet regimen can be a root cause of it, too. On the other, it has been discovered that these disorders can stem from when begin to feel overwhelmed, powerless, hurt and intimidated over time, which can be traced to one negative life experience or the other. Such runs deep and strongly affects our solar plexus chakra, since it is our power centre.

For instance, a patient of mine, who is also a law student suffered ulcer after failing his bar exams. The exam meant so much to him that he starved for days, while trying to process the painful experience. He eventually developed ulcer as a result. It also made him powerless as he questioned if he would pass next year.

Stress

CHAKRAS AFFECTED   *root chakra, the other chakras may be affected*

Stress is a term used to describe the state of the body after undergoing tension, emotional strain or hectic circumstances mostly caused by extremely demanding situations in our lives, work and relationships. As we undergo stress, our adrenals activate our stress hormone, which is cortisol, to step in and handle the situation. The adrenaline also functions as our flight or fight hormone. It works with the cortisol to relieve us for a while under stress. Their impacts are only effective for a short time; but, as stress prevails they have a way of wearing off. However, the presence of stress indicates that our root chakra is out of harmony. This makes us feel powerless and insecure about catering for our survival. We feel we may starve or die due to our inability to meet our needs. This consequently induces fear in us, thereby activating our survival instincts.

The presence of stress terribly affects the root chakra, and fear does the same to other chakras in the following ways:

- **Sacral plexus chakra:** Stress that stifle our ability to express ourselves creatively or sexually.

- **Root chakra:** Stress that makes us feel that our basic needs for survival are lacking.

- **Solar plexus chakra:** Stress that makes us feel powerless with low self-esteem.

- **Heart chakra:** Stress that makes us disconnect from ourselves and other as a result of past hurts.

- **Throat chakra:** Stress from not being able to communicate clearly or speak our truth.

- **Third eye chakra:** Stress that prevents us from being insightful or seeing the bigger side of things.

- **Crown chakra:** Stress that alienates us from the Divine and our spiritual selves.

Thyroid Disorders

<u>CHAKRA AFFECTED</u>   *throat chakra*

The throat is unique type of chakra that is basically concerned with how we communicate and speaking our truth. Essentially, the ideal way to honour our throat chakra is by unreservedly speaking our truths in ways it ought to be; that is, ways that represent who we are, how we feel and how we want to be heard.

However, when we have issues with our throats or necks, without any trace to trauma or physical injury, then it is a sign that our throat chakra is out of harmony. And, when this is the case, it is possible that we have learnt to silence ourselves or keep quiet over certain important issues that need expression such as abuse or hurt. It can also stem from overly keeping quiet over time, when there is so much that we want to say. Former patients of thyroid disorders got their healing from gradually expressing themselves about what they have longed to share. Interestingly, they have grown to become excellent communicators, who also guide victims of this ailment on the path of healing and release by sharing their own stories.

Uterine Fibroids and Cysts

CHAKRAS AFFECTED   *sacral plexus chakra*

Uterine fibroids are growths in the uterus that are commonly experienced by some women in childbearing years. They are non-cancerous. Interestingly, they do not show symptoms during their existence; but, are known to affect breathing and cause severe pains during childbirth, digestion and bowel movement. However, a cyst is an abnormal growth non-cancerous growth, filled with fluids; but, causes pain sometimes.

The presence of abnormal growths in the body such as fibroids and cysts suggest that the sacral plexus chakra is out of harmony. Thee growths causes blockages of sensitive areas in the body, consequently leading to drainage of energy within and slow creative flow. More so, other instances that can precipitate these growths include harbouring toxic thoughts, holding onto hurts and painful experiences that can be traceable to the family, work spaces, old relationships etc.

Weight Issues

One weight issue commonly experienced by some people is obesity. However, weight issues can be caused by dietary changes, exercise, lifestyle and behaviours; but, it has been observed that another cause of it can be traceable to not feeling grounded. Since our root chakra is related to our centre of power, the fact that we do no longer feel grounded in our spaces could be an indication that our root chakra is out of balance. Our root chakra makes us feel secured, powerful and connected to nature. A good sign of our root chakra being is in place is when we gain weight and look good.

Interestingly, our experiences play a great role on the state of our weights. Our weight tends to diminish when we are assaulted by life in form of attacks or intimidation, which makes us feel powerless or rubs off on our self-esteem. They cause our solar plexus chakra to go deeper out of harmony.

More so, we can be disconnected from our feelings in such a way that makes it difficult for us to experience pleasurable moments and express how we feel. We also bottle up our feelings, but ignore and not process them.

This indicates that our sacral plexus chakra is out of harmony.

This chapter focused at a long list of common symptoms and diseases that are experienced by people as well as the chakras directly linked to them. Going forward, we will be discussing the appropriate healing techniques for each of the chakras.

4

HEALING REMEDIES AND TREATMENTS

■■ ■■ ■■

For the sake of clarity, this chapter is divided into eight sections; the first seven sections are dedicated to each of the chakras, while the final one would be used to discuss healing techniques for multiple chakras. We will be practically looking at tested chakras that have been helpful to my patients, so far. I urge you to embrace these techniques as tools that will set you on the pathway of your healing journey.

THE ROOT CHAKRA

When we talk about being grounded, powerful and secure about all your needs for survival, the root chakra comes to mind. It is also concerned with feeling connected to your family and values in healthy ways. All these will be intact as long as the root chakra remains balanced. However, when it begins to go out of harmony the techniques for getting it back in shape include: meditation, crystal techniques, essential oil application and yoga postures. More so, it enables you to establish connection with the energy vortex, so that it can you can be ushered into the light and wisdom it has to offer.

Meditations

Here are valid practical meditation and visualisations steps to help connect with your root chakra:

1. Take three slow, deep breaths as you stay comfortably in a sitting or lying position. Imagine energy fusing through your perineum; that is, the space between the anus and genitals. Then as you exhale, try to release any energy held back in that area. It could be stress, pain, fear, insecurities, powerlessness etc. As you do this, you are releasing those toxic feelings into the atmosphere, thereby quickening the healing of your chakra.

2. Gently tap the sides of your lower hips; by doing so, you "wake up" the connection with the root chakra. This can also be achieved by slowly massaging the areas with both fingers.

3. With your steady breaths, inhaling and exhaling, continually direct your breaths to your root chakra. With eyes closed, picture a budding red light ahead of you, pulsing with life. If you are a male, make it whirl clockwise; if you are a female, make it whirl anti-clockwise.

4. Wait till you are settled into a calmer state, before engaging your root chakra. Ask it what it needs right now from you. Be attentive for any feedbacks as you keep breathing. Such can come in any form ranging from colour, sound, whispers, images, feelings, ideas etc. Be sure of your answers, before acting on them. If none is forthcoming, keep up with your practice. They will come later.

5. If you don't receive any answers from your chakra, do not worry. Instead, check to see, if there is any sensation around your lower hip region such as pulsations or vibration. If that is the case, you are connecting with your chakra!

6. As you conclude your meditation, take three slow, deep breaths, and inhale towards the direction of the ground or your feet.

7. *Caution!:* it is important that you are aware of the need to apply caution in this venture. There is a need to be slow and patient with yourself, because it takes time to cultivate. Do not outdo yourself. For instance, when you begin to feel pain at your lower back, it means you are stretching too much and should take a break as soon as possible, till you are energised. Note that during the course of your meditation, you will feel other thoughts invading your mind at some points to distract you.

Do not fret as this is commonly experienced by meditators around the world. Let these thoughts float around, and refuse to approach them with any judgements.

Crystals

For every chakra we have, there are crystals that resonate with them. For the root chakra we have: black tourmaline, hematite, obsidian, ruby, garnet, lodestone, smoky quartz, onyx, red jasper and fire agate.

How can you use crystals to connect with your root chakra? Firstly, make sure they are neat and cleansed from the energy of the former user, and ensure that your intentions for their usage are set.

Here we go:

- Smudging with white sage: Get your white sage ready. Light up the tip, till it starts beaming with smoke. Then blow out the flame, get the crystal that you are using, and hold it in the flame for a few seconds, knowing that you will use it to help you connect to your root chakra. This method is valid; because, just as you cleansed your crystals, you can equally cleanse your bodies by directing the smoke towards your chakras.
- Arrange them outside, overnight, to soak in the moonbeams and its energy.

- For cleaning purposes, run them over water or soak in salt. However, apply more caution when cleaning with water.

After cleaning and charging your crystal, here are few ways you can work with them:

- Lie or sit in a comfortable position. While at it, take hold of the crystal in your left hand. This will enable you to receive the healing energy of the crystal. Pay attention to how you feel, when you pick it up. Is it throbbing or pulsating in your hands? Do you feel vibrations? Any sensations? It is okay, if any of these is absent. While you await these sensations, it is important to note that it may take a while to feel awareness with a stone's energy. You need to patient. You can also ask your chakra for wisdom on how to go about this. Keep your mind open on feedbacks. Such can come in any form ranging from colours, sounds, whispers, images, feelings, memories, emotions, ideas and so on. Keep in mind that some crystals might require that you get used to them first, before opening up to you. And, when it happens, you are most likely to get an epiphany right there; but, until it comes, continue to remind yourself that you are one step closer to being connected to it. Show yourself kindness by being patient, instead of fretting over.

- However, you can decide to just go about it this way. Lie down in a comfortable position and place the stone on your pubic bone. Take three slow, deep breaths as if to say you are extracting the energy from the stone. Shortly, you may feel the energy in that area as stated in the preceding technique. It could be in form of vibrations, sensations, throbbing pulsations, a heartbeat, a light energy flowing across your lower hips etc. It is okay, if you do not feel any of these. In conclusion, if you want to intentionally connect more to your chakra, you might consider stating the words of affirmation on the last paragraph in the Essential Oils' section.

Essential Oils

There are various essential oils that correspond to the various chakras. Here are the ones that are related to the root chakra: vetiver, sandalwood, patchouli, spikenard and myrrh.

For the purpose of using the oils to connect to your chakra, here is how you can go about it. Get a container of oil; add about five or six drops to a dime-size portion of carrier oil. On the other hand, it is advisable to directly apply the oils on the chakras; but, due to the possibility of them being affected by your hands, it is better to activate the oils in another way.

As the oils get activated, put the mixture in your hand, and rub them together, causing a friction. When this is done, open your palms to release the scent and energy from the oils into the atmosphere, while deeply inhaling it. To get the energy to sink into your body, place your right hand on your pubic bone, and leave it there for a while. You can as well place both of your hands on the sides of your lower hips, and feel the energy reverberating through your soul.

Connecting with your root chakra is a very key goal in this venture. This is why you should be very intentionally, regardless of the strategies you are using for it; either by anointing your chakras directly or by rubbing them together on your palms. Finally, make a statement of affirmation that goes like this, "Today I come to create a connection with my root chakra. May my being and whole self be grounded and secured in this pursuit. I open up myself to release all embedded fears that threaten the peace of my existence. I ask to receive sufficient support in my drive to provide my daily needs; that I live in harmony and peaceful with my family, relations, tribal consciousness, that gives me room to float and flow with the motions of life. And so it is."

Yoga

Since the root chakra is our seat of power it is all about support and stability. The yoga style that corresponds to it are standing poses that strengthens the legs and enables it to stand firmly on the ground at any time. These poses include: Warrior I, Warrior II, Tree pose and Chair pose. However, some sitting poses are related to grounding as well such as Standing Forward Bend and Head-to-Knee Pose. They strongly help in balancing and ensure that the back of the leg is well stretched. Finally, restorative poses help us to surrender to the gravity and groundedness of the root chakra. They include: Reclining Bound Angle Pose, Supported Corpse Pose and Supported Child's pose.

(See the Appendix for illustrations.)

Other Tips

- Chant the mantra for this chakra named: "LAM."

- Eat root vegetables; it improves your grounding.

- Spend time in and around nature.

- Relish in doing activities that allows your bare feet to touch and feel the earth.

- Often stomp your feet to feel and connect with the earth.

- Learn to make pottery. (It will equally enhance your sacral plexus chakra.)

THE SACRAL PLEXUS CHAKRA

The sacral plexus chakra is basically concerned about connecting with your creative expressions, emotions, sexuality and abundance in ways that are pure and healthy. As we go further, we will look at how the following would help you connect to this chakra and how to equally establish connection with the energy vortex; so that it can you can be ushered into the light and wisdom it has to offer. They include: meditations, crystal techniques, essential oil applications and yoga postures.

Meditations

In this section, we will be looking at valid practical meditation and visualisations steps to help connect with your sacral plexus chakra:

1. Lie or sit in a comfortable position and take three, slow deep breaths. Any time you inhale, imagine energizing the two inches below your navel. Then as you exhale, try as much as you can to release anything being held back in that area. It could be fears, pain, insecurities or even expectations of how you are supposed to feel in this venture. This properly positions the connection of the chakra to take place. Then place your hand on your heart region to help facilitate speedy connection. Also, placing one hand on your heart chakra and the other on your sacral plexus chakra energizes the heart chakra and sacral plexus chakra at the same time.

2. Gently tap the two inches below the navel; by doing so, you "wake up" the connection with the root chakra. This can also be achieved by slowly massaging the areas with both fingers.

3. As you keep breathing, let energy through the sacral plexus chakra. Imagine a budding orange

sphere of light growing in that axis. Those that mostly identify with male and female energies should whirl it clockwise and anti-clockwise respectively.

4. Wait till you are settled into a calmer state, before engaging your sacral plexus chakra. Ask it what it needs right now from you. Be attentive for any feedbacks as you keep breathing. Such can come in any form ranging from colour, sound, whispers, images, feelings, ideas etc. Be sure of your answers, before acting on them. If none is forthcoming, keep up with your practice. They will come later.

5. If you don't receive any answers from your chakra, do not worry. Check to see, if you can feel any sensation such as pulsations or vibration. If that is the case, you are connecting with your chakra!

6. As you round off your meditation, take three, deep slow breaths, channelling your energy to the soles of your feet. Now open your eyes.

8. *Caution during meditation/visualisation:* the place of caution in this venture cannot be overemphasized. This demands patience on your own part. You know are you are pushing yourself too hard, when you begin to feel ache in your belly. Take a break and return to it, when you feel strong again. Also, note that during the course of

your meditation, you will feel other thoughts invading your mind at some points to distract you. Do not fret as this is commonly experienced by meditators around the world. Let these thoughts float around, and refuse to approach them with any judgements; then bring yourself back to the centre point.

Crystals

These are the crystals that resonate with the sacral plexus chakra: moonstone, amber, orange tourmaline, carnelian, sunstone etc.

The first thing to do when you are about to connect with your sacral plexus chakra is to ensure that these crystals are well cleansed. The idea is to wipe off the energies of its previous users to avoid issues. Also, make you sure that your mind is made up about your intention.

You can clean your crystals by:

- **Smudging:** Get your white sage ready. Light up the tip, till it starts beaming with smoke. Then blow out the flame, get the crystal that you are using, and hold it in the flame for a few seconds, knowing that you will use it to help you connect to your sacral chakra. This method is valid; because, just as you cleansed your crystals, you can equally cleanse your bodies by directing the smoke towards your chakras.

- Arrange them outside, overnight, to soak in the moonbeams and its energy.

- For cleaning purposes, run them over water or soak in salt. However, apply more caution when cleaning with water.

After you charged them up for use, these are ways in which you can make use of them.

- Lie or sit in a comfortable position. While at it, take hold of the crystal in your left hand. This will enable you to receive the healing energy of the crystal. Pay attention to how you feel, when you pick it up. Is it throbbing or pulsating in your hands? Do you feel vibrations? Any sensations? It is okay, if any of these is absent. While you await these sensations, it is important to note that it may take a while to feel awareness with a stone's energy. You need to patient. You can also ask your sacral plexus chakra for wisdom on how to go about this. Keep your mind open on feedbacks. Such can come in any form ranging from colours, sounds, whispers, images, feelings, memories, emotions, ideas and so on. Keep in mind that some crystals might require that you get used to them first, before opening up to you. And, when it happens, you are most likely to get an epiphany right there; but, until it comes, continue to remind yourself that you are one step closer to being connected to it. Show yourself kindness by being patient, instead of fretting over.

- As you are still lying down, pick your selected sacral plexus chakra crystals and place them some inches below your navel. Take three deep, slow breaths; this gives you room to drink the energies emanating from the crystals. The energy may notify you of its presence in various ways. It could come in form of a gentle heartbeat or pulsating sensations. You may also feel your energy interacting with that of the crystals. However, you may not necessarily feel any of these; and, it is okay, if you do not. To connect more intentionally with your chakra, consider saying the words of affirmation on the last paragraph of the Essential Oils' section.

Essential Oils

These are the essential oils that correspond with the sacral plexus chakra include: patchouli, rosewood, sandal wood and Ylang yland.

To connect with your chakra, you can make use of single oil or a mixture of them. When you are set, add a minimum of five and six max to a dime portion of carrier oil (like, jojoba oil). Apply it on a cotton ball, and touch it on the sacral plexus chakra, located some inches below the navel; also anoint yourself.

Alternatively, as the oils get activated, put the mixture in your hand, and rub them together, causing a friction. When this is done, open your palms to release the scent and energy from the oils into the atmosphere, while deeply inhaling it. To get the energy to sink into your body, place your right hand on your pubic bone, and leave it there for a while. You can as well place both of your hands on your chakra, and feel the energy reverberating through your soul. Regardless of how you go about it, the most important thing is to create a connection with your sacral plexus chakra.

After anointing yourself or inhaling scent of the activated oils in your palms, make an affirmative statement like this: "I now choose to establish a connection with my sacral plexus chakra. As I progress in this venture, May I be in touch with my emotions in healthy ways, express myself creatively to the world, connect to my pleasure, as well as the emotional aspects of my sexuality in ways that sustain me. I get rid of the fears that hinder me from connecting with my sexuality, abundance, creativity and emotions. I ask for support as I strive towards maintaining harmony in my emotions, in order to be at peace with how I feel. And so it is."

Yoga

We have already established the fact that there are different poses that correspond with each chakra. However, it is important to note that the sacral plexus chakra is the seat of our physical strength, and equally doubles as one for sweetness and creativity. Coming to the poses, it could be any that rejuvenates our core muscles, such as four limbed staff posture and all the warrior poses. Poses that nurture our creativity are the flowing movement and breath, Child pose—this promotes flexibility in the lower spine. We also have Happy Baby Pose and Downward Facing Dog. There are poses that are helpful in opening the hip and groin, such as Bound Angle Pose, Open Angel Pose, Cow Face Pose, and the Pigeon Pose—this entails a forward bending of the legs in the first stage. (See the Appendix, for the illustrations of the yoga poses.)

Other Tips

- Learn the basics of tantra to help you get more in touch with your sexuality on a conscious level.

- Chant the mantra sound that corresponds to this chakra: "VAM"

- Practice hula-hooping.

- Channel your emotions by trying your hands at forms of creative expressions such as writing, journaling, painting etc.

- Dance—it could be belly dancing or Latin dances such as salsa, and other dances that involve hip movements.

- Normalise constant playing. It will help you cultivate flexibility in learning how to experience pleasure and joy.

- Normalise expressing your emotions in healthy ways. Avoid toxic thoughts, people and spaces as they can influence your reactions to the things around you.

THE SOLAR PLEXUS CHAKRA

The solar plexus chakra basically has to do with your self-esteem, standing in your power and being in touch with your inner warrior fire. As usual, meditations, crystals techniques, essential oil applications and yoga postures are systems that will help you connect deeply with this chakra. Most importantly, it will initiate a sublime connection with the energy vortex within you to enable you open up to the light and wisdom it has to offer.

Meditations

In this section, we will be looking at valid cum verified practical meditation and visualisation steps to help connect with your solar plexus chakra:

1. As you sit or lie in a comfortable position, take three deep breaths. Any time you inhale, imagine the breath energizing the region above your navel. Each time you exhale, take time to wholly release whatever you could be holding back in that area—it could be pain, fears, hurting memories or even expectations of how you are supposed to feel. This properly positions the connection of the chakra to take place. Then place your hand on your heart region to help facilitate speedy connection. Also, placing one hand on your heart chakra and the other on your sacral plexus chakra energizes the heart chakra and sacral plexus chakra at the same time.

2. Gently tap the two inches below the navel; by doing so, you "wake up" the connection with the root chakra. This can also be achieved by slowly massaging the areas with both fingers in circular motion.

3. As you keep breathing, let the flow of the energy towards the solar plexus chakra. Imagine a budding yellow sphere of light growing in that axis. Those that mostly identify with male and female energies should whirl it clockwise and anti-clockwise respectively.

4. Wait till you are settled into a calmer state, before engaging your sacral plexus chakra. Ask it what it needs right now from you. Be attentive for any feedbacks as you keep breathing. Such can come in any form ranging from colour, sound, whispers, images, feelings, ideas etc. Be sure of your answers, before acting on them. If none is forthcoming, keep up with your practice. They will come later.

5. If you don't receive any answers from your chakra, do not worry. Check to see, if you can feel any sensation such as pulsations or vibration. If that is the case, you are connecting with your solar plexus chakra!

6. As you round off your meditation, take three, deep slow breaths, channelling your energy to the soles of your feet. Now open your eyes.

7. *Caution during meditation/visualisation:* the place of caution in this venture cannot be overemphasized. This demands patience on your

own part. You know are you are pushing yourself too hard, when you begin to feel ache in your belly. Take a break and return to it, when you feel strong again. Also, note that during the course of your meditation, you will feel other thoughts invading your mind at some points to distract you. Do not fret as this is commonly experienced by meditators around the world. Let these thoughts float around, and refuse to approach them with any judgements and draw yourself back to the centre.

Crystals

The crystals that resonate with the solar plexus chakra include yellow citrine, amber, yellow agate, yellow tiger's eye, yellow topaz and rutilated quartz. (See the Appendix for images of some of these crystals)

We have already established that very first thing to do, while connecting to your crystals is to thoroughly cleanse them of the energies of their former users. This is important to ensure smooth and stable connection. Also, have clarity about your intentions. This is how you clean your crystals:

- **Smudging:** Get your white sage ready. Light up the tip, till it starts beaming with smoke. Then blow out the flame, get the crystal that you are using, and hold it in the flame for a few seconds, knowing that you will use it to help you connect to your solar plexus chakra. This method is valid; because, just as you cleansed your crystals, you can equally cleanse your bodies by directing the smoke towards your chakras.

- Arrange them outside, overnight, to soak in the moonbeams and its energy.

- For cleaning purposes, run them over water or soak in salt. However, apply more caution when cleaning with water.

After cleaning your crystals, this is how you can work with them:

- Lie or sit in a comfortable position. While at it, take hold of the crystal in your left hand. This will enable you to receive the healing energy of the crystal. Pay attention to how you feel, when you pick it up. Is it throbbing or pulsating in your hands? Do you feel vibrations? Any sensations? It is okay, if any of these is absent. While you await these sensations, it is important to note that it may take a while to feel awareness with a stone's energy. You need to patient. You can also ask your solar plexus chakra for wisdom on how to go about this. Keep your mind open on feedbacks. Such can come in any form ranging from colours, sounds, whispers, images, feelings, memories, emotions, ideas and so on. Keep in mind that some crystals might require that you get used to them first, before opening up to you. And, when it happens, you are most likely to get an epiphany right there; but, until it comes, continue to remind yourself that you are one step closer to being connected to it. Show yourself kindness by being patient, instead of fretting over.

- As you are still lying down, pick your selected solar plexus chakra crystals and place them some inches above your navel. Take three deep, slow breaths; this gives you room to drink the energies emanating from the crystals. The energy may notify you of its presence in various ways. It could come in form of a gentle heartbeat or pulsating sensations. You may also feel your energy interacting with that of the crystals. However, you may not necessarily feel any of these; and, it is okay, if you do not. To connect more intentionally with your solar plexus chakra, consider saying the words of affirmation on the last paragraph of the Essential Oils' section.

Essential Oils

These are the essential oils that correspond with the solar plexus chakra include: lemon, rosemary, Roman chamomile and lavender.

To connect with your chakra, you can make use of single oil or a mixture of them. When you are set, add a minimum of five and six max to a dime portion of carrier oil (like, jojoba oil). Apply it on a cotton ball, and touch it on the solar plexus chakra, located some inches below the navel; also anoint yourself.

Alternatively, as the oils get activated, put the mixture in your hand, and rub them together, causing a friction. When this is done, open your palms to release the scent and energy from the oils into the atmosphere, while deeply inhaling it. You can as well place both of your hands on your chakra, and feel the energy reverberating through your soul. Regardless of how you go about it, the most important thing is to create a connection with your solar plexus chakra.

After anointing yourself or inhaling scent of the activated oils in your palms, make an affirmative statement like this: "I now choose to establish a connection with my solar plexus chakra. As I progress in this venture, May I understand my self-worth and personal power. I get rid of the fears that hinder me from connecting with my personal power and life's purpose. I ask for support as I strive towards maintaining harmony with my inner warrior, feel grounded, be myself and live my life confidently. And so it is."

Yoga

As we already know, the solar plexus chakra functions as the centre of personal power and confidence. So, in your yoga practice, you need poses that asks that your middle spine be flexible, requires much energy, makes you feel strong and quickens your inner warrior. Such poses include Cow Pose, Cat Pose, Sun Salutation, Boat Pose, or Half Pose. Other effective poses include: Breath of Fire or Bellows Breath and Leg lifts.

Here is a pertinent note about Breath of Fire or Bellows Breath: It is a unique type of pose as it has the ability to fire up metabolism and generate a lot of energy; so, you are advised to refrain from doing it before or close to bed time. *How is it performed?* It is performed through the nose, with the mouth closed. While inhaling is a core part of the process, the focus is mainly on exhaling, in which the breath is forced out by sharply drawing the abdomen in and up. This allows the air to forcefully escape through the lungs. The centre point of action stems from the navel which pumps in and out for inhalation and exhalation respectively. The difference between this practice and Breath of Fire is that the while the latter requires more rapidity, this focuses on rhythm and fullness.

Other Tips

- Put on yellow clothing

- Go out of your comfort zone and explore life. Such helps you grow your confidence and self-esteem.

- Undergo martial classes as it helps to strengthen your personal power.

- Chant the mantra sound that corresponds to this chakra: "RA"

- Establish healthy energy boundaries with those in your life as it would enable you strengthen your inner power. How do you go about this? Simply surround yourself in an egg of white light; this mostly applies to whenever you are in a toxic space or situation such as talking with a toxic co-worker, work space, dealing with social anxiety or entering a room full of people.

- Consider taking martial arts classes or practices as it help to strengthen your personal power.

THE HEART CHAKRA

The heart chakra is basically concerned about being connected with yourself. It also runs down to cultivating virtues such as self-love, compassion and joy. As usual, meditations, crystals techniques, essential oil applications and yoga postures are systems that will help you connect deeply with this chakra. Most importantly, it will initiate a sublime connection with the energy vortex within you to enable you open up to the light and wisdom it has to offer.

Meditations

In this section, we will be looking at valid cum verified practical meditation and visualisation steps to help connect with your heart chakra:

1. As you sit or lie in a comfortable position, take three deep breaths. Any time you inhale, imagine the breath energizing the region above your navel. Each time you exhale, take time to wholly release whatever you could be holding back in that area— it could be pain, fears, hurting memories or even expectations of how you are supposed to feel. This properly positions the connection of the heart chakra to take place.

2. How do you "wake up" the connection of this chakra? Gentle tap the centre of the chest or use your first two fingers to massage the axis in a circular motion.

3. As you keep breathing, let the flow of the energy be directed towards the heart chakra. Imagine a budding green sphere of light growing in that axis, pulsing and expanding. Those that mostly identify with female and male energies should whirl it clockwise and anti-clockwise respectively.

4. Wait till you are settled into a calmer state, before engaging your heart chakra. Ask it what it needs right now from you. Be attentive for any feedbacks as you keep breathing. Such can come in any form ranging from colour, sound, whispers, images, feelings, ideas etc. Be sure of your answers, before acting on them. If none is forthcoming, keep up with your practice. They will come later.

5. If you don't readily receive any answers from your chakra, do not worry. Check to see, if you can feel any awareness such as pulsations, vibrations or expanding sensations in your chest region. If that is the case, you are connecting with your heart chakra!

6. As you round off your meditation, take three, deep slow breaths, channelling your energy to the soles of your feet. Now gently open your eyes.

7. *Caution when doing this meditation/visualisation:* As you proceed in this venture, it is important that you are patient with yourself, because this meditation takes time to cultivate. You know are you are pushing yourself too hard, when your pulsations are running too fast. Take a break and return to it, when you feel strong again. Also, note that during the course of your meditation, you will feel other thoughts invading your mind at some points to distract you. Do not fret as this is commonly experienced by meditators around the

world. Let these thoughts float around, and refuse to approach them with any judgements and draw yourself back to the centre.

Crystals

The crystals that resonate with the solar plexus chakra include: emerald, green tourmaline, jade, green calcite, green kyanite rose quartz and peridot. (See the Appendix for images of some of these crystals)

The first step to take while connecting your crystals with your heart chakra is to clean them up. This is important so that the energies of its former users will not be mashed up with yours. Also, get clarity on what your intentions are. This is how you clean your crystals:

- **Smudging:** Get your white sage ready. Light up the tip, till it starts beaming with smoke. Then blow out the flame, get the crystal that you are using, and hold it in the flame for a few seconds, knowing that you will use it to help you connect to your heart chakra. This method is valid; because, just as you cleansed your crystals, you can equally cleanse your bodies by directing the smoke towards your chakras.

- Arrange them outside, overnight, to soak in the moonbeams and its energy.
- For cleaning purposes, run them over water or soak in salt. However, apply more caution when cleaning with water. Any of the stones that rates low on the Moh hardness scale is at a high risk of being damaged.

After cleaning your crystals, this is how you can work with them:

- Lie or sit in a comfortable position. While at it, take hold of the crystal in your left hand. This will enable you to receive the healing energy of the crystal. Pay attention to how you feel, when you pick it up. Is it throbbing or pulsating in your hands? Do you feel vibrations? Any sensations? It is okay, if any of these is absent. While you await these sensations, it is important to note that it may take a while to feel awareness with a stone's energy. You need to patient. You can also ask your heart chakra for wisdom on how to go about this. Keep your mind open on feedbacks. Such can come in any form ranging from colours, sounds, whispers, images, feelings, memories, emotions, ideas and so on. Keep in mind that some crystals might require that you get used to them first, before opening up to you. And, when it happens, you are most likely to get an epiphany right there; but, until it comes, continue to remind yourself that you are one step closer to being connected to it.

Show yourself kindness by being patient, instead of fretting over.

- As you lie down, place your preferred heart chakra crystal at the centre of your chest. Take three deep slow breaths; then allow yourself to digest the crystal's energy. As you hold onto your crystal, may feel the energy expanding within your heart in the form of a sensation or awareness. You may also feel your energy interacting with that of the crystals. However, you may not necessarily feel any of these; and, it is okay, if you do not. To connect more intentionally with your heart chakra, consider saying the words of affirmation on the last paragraph of the Essential Oils' section.

Essential Oils

These are the essential oils that correspond with the heart chakra include: geranium, rose, palmarosa, bergamot, lavender, ylang ylang and melissa/lemon balm.

To connect with your chakra, you can make use of single oil or a mixture of them. When you are set, add a minimum of five and six max to a dime portion of carrier oil (like, jojoba oil). Apply it on a cotton ball, and touch it on the heart chakra, located some inches below the navel; also anoint yourself.

Alternatively, as the oils get activated, put the mixture in your hand, and rub them together, causing a friction. When this is done, open your palms to release the scent and energy from the oils into the atmosphere, while deeply inhaling it. You can as well place both of your hands on your chakra, and feel the energy reverberating through your soul. Regardless of how you go about it, the most important thing is to create a connection with your heart chakra.

After anointing yourself or inhaling scent of the activated oils in your palms, make an affirmative statement like this: "I now intend to create a connection with my heart chakra. May I fully and completely connect with myself in loving and compassionate ways, and do the same to those around me. I get rid of all the fears that keep me from receiving and giving love. I request for support in transcending the vibration of my heart to one of joy. May I continually accept, appreciate and love myself, including my flaws. And so it is."

Yoga

The heart chakra doubles as the heart centre and the seat of our souls. However, certain yoga poses can be instrumental in opening up this area of our bodies. They include: Camel Pose, Chest openers, such as Seated Spinal Twist. We also have the Eagle Pose which is really helpful for the backside of this chakra. More so, try arm balances; they are good for your heart, help you maintain stability, and enable your dreams and wishes take flight. (See Appendix for illustrations of yoga poses)

Other Tips

- Chant the mantra sound that corresponds to this chakra: "YUM"

- Cultivate and practice the virtue of forgiveness—towards yourself and others.

- Be open to showing genuine love and affection towards those you love.

- Get a bouquet of roses for yourself. Roses resonate with the heart chakra.

- Prepare a rosebud tea for yourself. You can buy them from herb shops or specialty tea shops. Interestingly, they abound in many food stores and Asian markets; also, they basically originate from a Chinese medicinal herb called *mei gui hua*. This is how you go about it: steep a few buds in a large mug of hot water for just a few minutes. Then, create a love ritual for yourself, ingesting the love of the roses.

THE THROAT CHAKRA

The throat chakra basically has to do with speaking your truth, being true to yourself, effectively communicating your needs and expressing yourself. As we proceed, we would be looking at meditations, crystal techniques, essential oil applications and yoga postures that will help you connect deeply with this chakra. Most importantly, it will initiate a sublime connection with the energy vortex within you to enable you open up to the light and wisdom it has to offer.

Meditations

In this section, we will be looking at valid cum verified practical meditation and visualisation steps to help connect with your throat chakra:

1. As you sit or lie in a comfortable position, take three deep breaths. Any time you inhale, imagine the breath energizing the region above your navel. Each time you exhale, take time to wholly release whatever you could be holding back in that area—it could be pain, fears, hurting memories or even expectations of how you are supposed to feel. Try placing your hand on your chest region. It actually positions the connection of the chakra to take place.

2. How do you "wake up" the connection of this chakra? Gentle tap the bone in front of the notch at the front of your throat or use your first two fingers to massage the axis in a circular motion.

3. As you keep breathing, let the flow of the energy be directed towards the throat chakra. Imagine a budding blue sphere of light growing in that axis, pulsing and expanding. Those that mostly identify with male and female energies should whirl the sphere clockwise and anti-clockwise respectively.

4. Wait till you are settled into a calmer state, before engaging your throat chakra. Ask it what it needs right now from you. Be attentive for any feedbacks as you keep breathing. Such can come in any form ranging from colour, sound, whispers, images, feelings, ideas etc. Be sure of your answers, before acting on them. If none is forthcoming, keep up with your practice. They will come later.

5. If you don't readily receive any answers from your chakra, do not worry. Check to see, if you can feel any awareness such as pulsations, widening or expanding sensations in your throat region. If that is the case, you are connecting with your heart chakra!

6. As you round off your meditation, take three, deep slow breaths, channelling your energy to the soles of your feet. Now gently open your eyes.

8. *Caution when doing this meditation/visualisation:* As you proceed in this venture, it is important that you are patient with yourself, because this meditation takes time to cultivate. You know are you are pushing yourself too hard, when you begin to feel ache in your neck. Take a break and return to it, when you feel strong again. Also, note that during the course of your meditation, you will feel other thoughts invading your mind at some points to distract you. Do not fret as this is commonly

experienced by meditators around the world. Let these thoughts float around, and refuse to approach them with any judgements and draw yourself back to the centre.

Crystals

The crystals that resonate with the throat chakra include: sodalite, celestite, aquamarine, iolite, blue kyanite, turquoise and lapis lazuli. (See the Appendix for images of some of these crystals)

The first step to take while connecting your crystals with your throat chakra is to clean them up. This is important so that the energies of its former users will not be mashed up with yours. Also, get clarity on what your intentions are. This is how you clean your crystals:

- **Smudging:** Get your white sage ready. Light up the tip, till it starts beaming with smoke. Then blow out the flame, get the crystal that you are using, and hold it in the flame for a few seconds, knowing that you will use it to help you connect to your throat chakra. This method is valid; because, just as you cleansed your crystals, you can equally cleanse your bodies by directing the smoke towards your chakras.

- Arrange them outside, overnight, to soak in the moonbeams and its energy.
- For cleaning purposes, run them over water or soak in salt. However, apply more caution when cleaning with water. Any of the stones that rates

low on the Moh hardness scale is at a high risk of being damaged.

After cleaning your crystals, this is how you can work with them:

- Lie or sit in a comfortable position. While at it, take hold of the crystal in your left hand. This will enable you to receive the healing energy of the crystal. Pay attention to how you feel, when you pick it up. Is it throbbing or pulsating in your hands? Do you feel vibrations? Any static prickles? It is okay, if any of these is absent. While you await these sensations, it is important to note that it may take a while to feel awareness with a stone's energy. You need to patient. You can also ask your throat chakra for wisdom on how to go about this. Keep your mind open on feedbacks. Such can come in any form ranging from colours, sounds, whispers, images, feelings, memories, emotions, ideas and so on. Keep in mind that some crystals might require that you get used to them first, before opening up to you. And, when it happens, you are most likely to get an epiphany right there; but, until it comes, continue to remind yourself that you are one step closer to being connected to it. Show yourself kindness by being patient, instead of fretting over.

- As you lie down, place your preferred throat chakra crystal at the centre of your chest. Take three deep slow breaths; then allow yourself to digest the crystal's energy. As you hold onto your crystal, may feel the energy expanding around your neck in the form of a sensation or awareness. You may also feel your energy interacting with that of the crystals. However, you may not necessarily feel any of these; and, it is okay, if you do not. To connect more intentionally with your throat chakra, consider saying the words of affirmation on the last paragraph of the Essential Oils' section.

Essential Oils

These are the essential oils that correspond with the throat chakra include: rosemary, frankincense, lavender, German chamomile and hyssop.

To connect with your chakra, you can make use of single oil or a mixture of them. When you are set, add a minimum of five and six max to a dime portion of carrier oil (like, jojoba oil). Apply it on a cotton ball, and touch it on the throat plexus chakra, located some inches below the navel; also anoint yourself.

Alternatively, as the oils get activated, put the mixture in your hand, and rub them together, causing a friction. When this is done, open your palms to release the scent and energy from the oils into the atmosphere, while deeply inhaling it. You can as well place both of your hands on your chakra, and feel the energy reverberating through your soul. Regardless of how you go about it, the most important thing is to create a connection with your throat chakra.

After anointing yourself or inhaling scent of the activated oils in your palms, make an affirmative statement like: "I now choose to create a connection with my throat chakra. May I be in harmony with my will to live, and may I continually be open to speak my truth authentically, creatively and easily. I release and resist the fears that hinder me from listening to my inner voice. Lastly, I request for support to consistently communicate freely and eventually be heard. And so it is."

Yoga

The throat chakra is basically centred on speaking your truth. So, the flexibility of our necks plays a vital role here. The stiffness of the neck could be an indication that the throat chakra is out harmony, thereby making us to relent in communicating effectively. A lot of poses are known as drishti; this means that they have a specific focal point in which the head follows the eyes, and the body follows the head. Some of these great yoga poses include: Warrior II, Camel Pose, Bridge Pose, Triangle Pose, Extended Side Angle, Shoulder stand and Plow Pose. Other postures that can involve twisting can aid the throat chakra. (See Appendix page for illustration of yoga poses).

Other Tips

- Put on light blue colour.

- Chant the mantra sound that corresponds to this chakra: "HUM"

- Practice singing, reading aloud, chanting or humming.

- Say what you are sure of, and be sure of what you say.

- Take teas that soothe the throat, such as spearmint, slippery elm and peppermint.

THE THIRD EYE CHAKRA

The throat chakra basically has to do with trusting your intuition and inner vision. As we proceed, we would be looking at meditations, crystal techniques, essential oil applications and yoga postures that will help you connect deeply with this chakra. Most importantly, it will initiate a sublime connection with the energy vortex within you to enable open up to the light and wisdom it has to offer.

If you want to enhance your connection with your third eye chakra, ensure that you drink unfluoridated water. It has been observed that fluoride calcifies the pineal gland, which is close related to the third eye. For this to be achieved, have a water purification system in place to enable you drink clean water always.

Meditations

In this section, we will be looking at valid cum verified practical meditation and visualisation steps to help connect with your third eye chakra:

1. As you sit or lie in a comfortable position, take three deep breaths. Any time you inhale, imagine the breath energizing the region above your navel. Each time you exhale, take time to wholly release whatever you could be holding back in that area—it could be pain, fears, hurting memories or even expectations of how you are supposed to feel. Try placing your hand on your chest region. It actually positions the connection of the chakra to take place.

2. How do you "wake up" the connection of this chakra? Gentle tap the area between your eyebrows our gently use your first two fingers to massage the axis in a circular motion.

3. As you keep breathing, let the flow of the energy be directed towards the throat chakra. Imagine a budding indigo sphere of light growing in that axis, pulsing and expanding. Those that mostly identify with female and male energies should

whirl the sphere clockwise and anti-clockwise respectively.

4. Wait till you are settled into a calmer state, before engaging your third eye chakra. Ask it what it needs right now from you. Be attentive for any feedbacks as you keep breathing. Such can come in any form ranging from colour, sound, whispers, images, feelings, ideas etc. Be sure of your answers, before acting on them. If none is forthcoming, keep up with your practice. They will come later.

5. If you don't readily receive any answers from your chakra, do not worry. Check to see, if you can feel any awareness such as pulsations, gentle ache or a thumb is being pressed around that region of your head. If that is the case, you are connecting with your third eye chakra!

6. As you round off your meditation, take three, deep slow breaths, channelling your energy to the soles of your feet. Now gently open your eyes.

7. *Caution when doing this meditation/visualisation:* As you proceed in this venture, it is important that you are patient with yourself, because this meditation takes time to cultivate. You know are you are pushing yourself too hard, when you begin to feel ache in your neck. Take a break and return to it, when you feel strong again. Also, note that

during the course of your meditation, you will feel other thoughts invading your mind at some points to distract you. Do not fret as this is commonly experienced by meditators around the world. Let these thoughts float around, and refuse to approach them with any judgements and draw yourself back to the centre.

Crystals

The crystals that resonate with the third eye chakra include: fluorite, lepidolite, sugilite, amethyst, tanzanite, lapis lazuli, clear quartz and star sapphire. (See the Appendix for images of some of these crystals)

The first step to take while connecting your crystals with your throat chakra is to clean them up. This is important so that the energies of its former users will not be mashed up with yours. Also, get clarity on what your intentions are. This is how you clean your crystals:

- **Smudging:** Get your white sage ready. Light up the tip, till it starts beaming with smoke. Then blow out the flame, get the crystal that you are using, and hold it in the flame for a few seconds, knowing that you will use it to help you connect to your third eye chakra. This method is valid; because, just as you cleansed your crystals, you can equally cleanse your bodies by directing the smoke towards your chakras.

- Arrange them outside, overnight, to soak in the moonbeams and its energy.
- For cleaning purposes, run them over water or soak in salt. However, apply more caution when cleaning with water. Any of the stones that rates low on the Moh hardness scale is at a high risk of being damaged.

After cleaning your crystals, this is how you can work with them:

- Lie or sit in a comfortable position. While at it, take hold of the crystal in your left hand. This will enable you to receive the healing energy of the crystal. Pay attention to how you feel, when you pick it up. Is it throbbing or pulsating in your hands? Do you feel vibrations? Any static prickles? It is okay, if any of these is absent. While you await these sensations, it is important to note that it may take a while to feel awareness with a stone's energy. You need to patient. You can also ask your third eye chakra for wisdom on how to go about this. Keep your mind open on feedbacks. Such can come in any form ranging from colours, sounds, whispers, images, feelings, memories, emotions, ideas and so on. Keep in mind that some crystals might require that you get used to them first, before opening up to you. And, when it happens, you are most likely to get an epiphany right there; but, until it comes, continue to remind yourself that you are one step closer to being connected to it. Show yourself kindness by being patient, instead of fretting over.

- As you lie down, place your preferred third eye chakra crystal on the space between your eyebrows. Take three deep slow breaths; then allow yourself to digest the crystal's energy. As

174

you hold onto your crystal, may feel the energy expanding in the space between your eyebrows in the form of a sensation or awareness. You may also feel your energy interacting with that of the crystals. However, you may not necessarily feel any of these; and, it is okay, if you do not. To connect more intentionally with your third eye chakra, consider saying the words of affirmation on the last paragraph of the Essential Oils' section.

Essential Oils

The essential oils that correspond with the third eye chakra include: frankincense, sandalwood and lavender.

To connect with your chakra, you can make use of single oil or a mixture of them. When you are set, add a minimum of five and six max to a dime portion of carrier oil (like, jojoba oil). Apply it on a cotton ball, and touch it on the third eye chakra, located some inches below the navel; also anoint yourself.

Alternatively, as the oils get activated, put the mixture in your hand, and rub them together, causing a friction. When this is done, open your palms to release the scent and energy from the oils into the atmosphere, while deeply inhaling it. You can as well place both of your hands on your chakra, and feel the energy reverberating through your soul. Regardless of how you go about it, the most important thing is to create a connection with your third eye chakra.

After anointing yourself or inhaling scent of the activated oils in your palms, make an affirmative statement like this: "I now intend to create a third eye connection with my third eye chakra. I equally get rid and resist all fears that hinder me from trusting my intuition. May I trust and follow it, and see beyond the physical realities before me, so that I may see all the possibilities coming to me, without difficulties. May I successfully apply the wisdom from my inner vision into all other aspects of my life, and continually support me as I connect with the emotional intelligence of my third eye. And so it is."

Yoga

The ideal focus of the third eye chakra is to see things from all angles/perspectives and beyond—all poses right-side up, upside down, twisted or eyes closed. After a while, try to experience *pratyahara* by wearing a blindfold during a set of poses. This actually helps to direct your vision more deeply into yourself or makes you more introspective, per say. More so, this chakra can be stimulated by other poses, such as doing supported Forward Bends using a blanket or extra bolster. (See Appendix page for illustration of yoga poses).

Other Tips

- Chant the mantra sound: "SHAM"

- Put on dark blue and indigo colours on your wardrobe.

- Ensure that your diet is free from fluoride by using a water purification system. This is because water purifies the pineal gland which is directly linked to the third eye chakra.

- Act on your intuition as soon as you get a hint. It will strengthen your intuition.

- Begin to eat foods, such as blueberries, blackberries, eggplant, prunes, beets, black currants and rainbow chard.

- Have clarity on the intentions that you want to achieve with your inner wisdom.

THE CROWN CHAKRA

The crown chakra is basically concerned about our spirituality; that is, becoming more connected with our Inner Divine, as well as how we are connected to the Divine. As we proceed, the following meditations, crystal techniques, essential oil applications and yoga postures will help you connect deeply with this chakra. Most importantly, it will initiate a sublime connection with the energy vortex within you to enable you open up to the light and wisdom it has to offer.

Meditation

In this section, we will be looking at valid cum verified practical meditation and visualisation steps to help connect with your third eye chakra:

1. As you sit or lie in a comfortable position, take three deep breaths. Any time you inhale, imagine the breath energizing the region above your navel. Each time you exhale, take time to wholly release whatever you could be holding back in that area—it could be pain, fears, hurting memories or even expectations of how you are supposed to feel. Try placing your hand on your chest region. It actually positions the connection of the chakra to take place.

2. How do you "wake up" the connection of this chakra? Gentle tap the area between your eyebrows our gently use your first two fingers to massage the axis in a circular motion.

3. As you keep breathing, let the flow of the energy be directed towards the crown chakra. Imagine a budding purple (or white or gold) sphere of light growing in that axis, pulsing and expanding. Those that mostly identify with male and female energies should whirl the sphere clockwise and counter-clockwise respectively.

4. Wait till you are settled into a calmer state, before engaging your crown chakra. Ask it what it needs right now from you. Be attentive for any feedbacks as you keep breathing. Such can come in any form ranging from colour, sound, whispers, images, feelings, ideas etc. Be sure of your answers, before acting on them. If none is forthcoming, keep up with your practice. They will come later.

5. If you don't readily receive any answers from your chakra, do not worry. Check to see, if you can feel any awareness such as pulsations, gentle ache or a thumb is being pressed around that region of your head. If that is the case, you are connecting with your crown chakra!

6. As you round off your meditation, take three, deep slow breaths, channelling your energy to the soles of your feet. Now gently open your eyes.

7. *Caution when doing this meditation/visualisation:* As you proceed in this venture, it is important that you are patient with yourself, because this meditation takes time to cultivate. You know are you are pushing yourself too hard, when you begin to feel a vertex headache or headache situated at the top of your head. Take a break and return to it, when you feel strong again. Also, note that during the course of your meditation, you will feel other thoughts invading your mind at some points to

distract you. Do not fret as this is commonly experienced by meditators around the world. Let these thoughts float around, and refuse to approach them with any judgements and draw yourself back to the centre.

Crystals

The crystals that resonate with the crown chakra include: clear quartz, Heckimer diamond, labradorite, moonstone, selenite, phenacite, kunzite, apophyllite, white topaz and amethyst. (See the Appendix for images of some of these crystals)

The first step to take while connecting your crystals with your crown chakra is to clean them up. This is important so that the energies of its former users will not be mashed up with yours. Also, get clarity on what your intentions are. This is how you clean your crystals:

- **Smudging:** Get your white sage ready. Light up the tip, till it starts beaming with smoke. Then blow out the flame, get the crystal that you are using, and hold it in the flame for a few seconds, knowing that you will use it to help you connect to your crown chakra. This method is valid; because, just as you cleansed your crystals, you can equally cleanse your bodies by directing the smoke towards your chakras.

- Arrange them outside, overnight, to soak in the moonbeams and its energy.
- For cleaning purposes, run them over water or soak in salt. However, apply more caution when cleaning with water. Any of the stones that rates

low on the Moh hardness scale is at a high risk of being damaged.

After cleaning your crystals, this is how you can work with them:

- Lie or sit in a comfortable position. While at it, take hold of the crystal in your left hand. This will enable you to receive the healing energy of the crystal. Pay attention to how you feel, when you pick it up. Is it throbbing or pulsating in your hands? Do you feel vibrations? Any static prickles? It is okay, if any of these is absent. While you await these sensations, it is important to note that it may take a while to feel awareness with a stone's energy. You need to patient. You can also ask your crown chakra for wisdom on how to go about this. Keep your mind open on feedbacks. Such can come in any form ranging from colours, sounds, whispers, images, feelings, memories, emotions, ideas and so on. Keep in mind that some crystals might require that you get used to them first, before opening up to you. And, when it happens, you are most likely to get an epiphany right there; but, until it comes, continue to remind yourself that you are one step closer to being connected to it. Show yourself kindness by being patient, instead of fretting over.

- As you lie down, place your preferred crown chakra crystal at the top centre of your head. Take three deep slow breaths; then allow yourself to digest the crystal's energy. As you hold onto your crystal, may feel the energy expanding in the space between your eyebrows in the form of a sensation or awareness. You may also feel your energy interacting with that of the crystals. However, you may not necessarily feel any of these; and, it is okay, if you do not. To connect more intentionally with your crown chakra, consider saying the words of affirmation on the last paragraph of the Essential Oils' section.

Essential Oils

The essential oils that correspond with the crown chakra include: peppermint, sandalwood, frankincense and lotus.

To connect with your chakra, you can make use of single oil or a mixture of them. When you are set, add a minimum of five and six max to a dime portion of carrier oil (like, jojoba oil). Apply it on a cotton ball, and touch it on the crown chakra, located some inches below the navel; also anoint yourself.

Alternatively, as the oils get activated, put the mixture in your hand, and rub them together, causing a friction. When this is done, open your palms to release the scent and energy from the oils into the atmosphere, while deeply inhaling it. You can as well place both of your hands on your chakra, and feel the energy reverberating through your soul. Regardless of how you go about it, the most important thing is to create a connection with your crown chakra.

After anointing yourself or inhaling scent of the activated oils in your palms, make an affirmative statement like this: "Now I intend to create a connection with my crown chakra. May I embrace the fact that a true reflection of the Divine/God/dess/Source/Universe. I totally get rid of or resist the fear that hinders me from trusting my path. I request to be supported in the increase of my consciousness, so that I may live in the knowledge of Unity, and trust that my life is turning out as it should. And so it is."

Yoga

Poses abound to help cultivate the crown chakra with yoga. The first is headstands. They play a vital role in making you ready to received information or messages from the Divine; this occurs when there is smooth flow of blood to the head. On the other hand, it is important to take caution in this venture. This is actually because beginners or amateurs are at a higher risk of incurring neck or shoulder injuries. If you are in such category, you are advised to practice under the watch and guidance of a trained yoga teacher. For more balancing of this chakra, meditation is highly recommended as a key factor in this venture.

Other Tips

- Put on the colour purple or white.

- Cultivate meditation or mindfulness.

- Begin to practice gratitude.

- Chant the mantra sound: "OM"

- Have clarity on the intention that you are in touch with your crown chakra, the Divine within yourself, and the Divine/Source/Universe/God/dess.

HEALING MULTIPLE CHAKRAS

Our chakra systems are well connected, just like everything on earth is. This is why they need to be in harmony to function well. In other words, an imbalance in one chakra can have a distressing effect on the others.

For instance, one of my patients named Miss Jane came to my office earlier to treat her cervical dysplasia. She suffered emotional unavailability from her parents as she grew from childhood into adulthood. Her father, who was always distant, never helped matters. He treated her in harsh ways that crumpled her self-esteem by making her feel ashamed of her adolescent body. In her bid to get her father's approval, she started taking desperate measures to change her situation. They include developing an eating disorder to control her weight, taking abusive substances, and started leading an unhealthy lifestyle.

Miss Jane's experience reveals her root chakra was in disharmony; and, this originated from the emotionally unavailability and feeling of neglect she suffered earlier by her family. This imbalance eventually grew to affect her power centre; that is, her solar plexus chakra. She was pressured in her self-worth and self-confidence, and this was what prompted her to correct this by developing eating disorders.

Interestingly, other chakras began to lose their impacts gradually. Miss Jane grew to mistrust her inner wisdom, her third eye chakra, and eventually unknowingly extended the silence of her throat chakra that she had felt growing up. Her sacral plexus chakra began to lose its touch, manifesting feelings of shame. Eventually, she started seeking for available ways to restore her self-esteem, emotions, personal relationship, and also started developing healthy habits. The state of disharmony of her numerous chakras disturbing often left shaken and vulnerable, but it never deterred her commitment towards healing and personal growth.

She also hugely invested in self-love and this played a huge role in her growth. Also, other factors were instrumental such as receiving Reiki treatments during her visits, working with crystals, essential oils and mindsets shifts sessions. Miss Jane's experience significantly tells us that no matter how broken we are, we need to be patient in our healing process, because it takes time.

Healing many chakras at the same time is possible; but, would only take time. Let us look at how to make use of crystals, breath work, visualisations, essential oils, and yoga to work on multiple chakras.

Meditation

The first step is to lie down in a comfortable position. Then relax and inhale deeply, gradually directing your breath to your root chakra. Do this for three more times as you allow yourself to release everything you have held onto in that chakra. You may want to place your hand in the lower region of your hips as you continue this exercise. Also, allow yourself to get in touch with the emotions stored up in that chakra. Alternatively, check to see, if there is any physical discomfort; most importantly, take note of anything you are sensing there. Now imagine a red sphere of light at the chakra—see it whirling, spinning and pulsing. Equally imagine that it gets more intense, grows and radiates light of healing onto your chakra. Observe if the sensations you felt are the still after the breath works and visualisations. Repeat this exercise for all the chakras, with their corresponding locations, colours and end at the crown chakra.

Crystals

If you are with your crystal stones, you can turn the previous exercise into a crystal bath. This is how you go about it: before you start working through the breathing exercises, place the crystals for each chakra on top of each other.

Alternatively, you can administer healing to all chakras by using a single crystal. For instance, Selenite is a very unique crystal—one that wipes off stains or unwanted impact in the energy body, and helps you to overcome the things holds you back from communicating with your Higher Self. Although selenite may come in many forms, you can utilise its wand form to address multiple chakras. How do you go about it? Place it on the midline of your body, or wherever it feels right in that region. For a better and balanced placement, place it in such a way that touches your heart chakra, solar plexus chakra, and if extended long enough, the sacral plexus chakra. The result is unique, when you utilise the selenite wand in this way. It eventually creates an energetic alignment or harmony with all the chakras; even those it is not physically touching.

Essential Oils

Essential oils can also be used to heal multiple chakras simultaneously. How do you go about this? anoint each chakra with a single or more oil used to reach one. Start with the root chakra and run your way down to the crown chakra. Anoint the specific chakras you want to anoint. On the other hand, try blending a couple of essential oils that have the capacity to treat many multiples chakras at once. At the end of the day, when working with essential oils, it is important that you make use a carrier oil, to avoid skin irritation.

Yoga

The yoga remains a unique healing technique for all the chakras. Its goal is to unite the breath with thorough bodily movements and awareness. A single yoga class or practice can be used to heal multiple chakras simultaneously. While at it, getting into specific poses and infusing breath can open up multiple energy centres at the same time.

(See appendix for illustrations of yoga poses).

YOGA POSES

The following yoga poses can be helpful or play a key role in helping to balancing your chakras. When you get to yoga poses that require you engage one side of the side of the body, practice the same pose with the other side body, too. The idea of this is to maintain balance and symmetry.

BOAT POSE

Start by sitting with your knees bent together, and your shins parallel to the ground. Now lift your chest to enable you maintain a long spine. Energetically stretch your hands in a forward manner in the direction of your knees. If you want to advance, straighten your legs and lift your feet forward.

BOUND ANGLE POSE

Begin by staying in a sitting position
 with both soles of your feet
pressed together. Lengthen your spine.
Lean forward, and try to reach
 your forehead towards your toes.

BRIDGE POSE

As you lie in a comfortable position,
 engage your abdomen and pelvic
floor muscles, with knees and hip-width
apart. Draw your heels your head
in an energetic manner and
press your feet downward.
Now raise your hips up.

CAMEL POSE

Begin by kneeling in a position
that allows you to place your
knees hip-width apart. Now
place your hands on your lower
back, with your fingers pointing
upward. Draw your palms
downward energetically to lengthen
your spine. Lift your heart
towards the sky. Finally, if you
want to advance, try to hold
your heels with your hands.

CAT POSE

Begin by kneeling in a tabletop
position. Elevate your spine
towards the sky, and tuck the
chin and tailbone under. Now
draw your navel in and up
towards the spine.

CHAIR POSE

Begin by standing with your feet
together, with your weight on
the heels. Now move your hips
downward, Sweep your
hands towards the sky, while
maintaining a neutral spine.

CHILD'S POSE

Begin this, too, in a tabletop position.
Lower your hips to touch your heels.
Now stretch your arms backward
towards your feet, alongside your
body, with your palms facing
upwards. Finally, rest your head
on the floor and relax for a while.

COW FACE POSITION

Begin by sitting tall, with your right knee stacked atop the other and hips laterally rotated. Ensure that your sitz bones should remain grounded. Now get your right hand behind your head, and your left hand behind your back. Try to hold both together in that position. *If your shoulders are stiff*: Reach both hands using a towel or yoga strap.

COW POSE

Begin again by staying a tabletop position. Put your back in an arch-like position as you drop your belly downward. Maintain throughout your spine. Look upwards and position the crown of your head towards the sky.

DOWNWARD FACING DOG

Begin this pose by staying in a
plank position. Place your ten
fingers towards on the ground
as you raise your hips skyward.
Shrink your shoulders, then move
 your chest towards your thighs,
and tuck your navel in. Now stretch
your legs in a lengthened form and reach
 down with your heels. Lastly, stay
 awhile and feel the many
opposing directional pulls.

EAGLE POSE

Begin this pose by staying in a Chair
Pose. Bind your hands and legs
in a knot. Now lengthen your spine,
and sink deeply into your knees.
Broaden your shoulders and lean
your hips forward. *If your shoulders
are stiff*: Give yourself a bear hug.
If your hips are stiff: Just give the
 legs a single wrap, and energetically
 intend towards a double bind.

EXTENDED SIDE ANGLE

Begin in a Warrior II position on the
right side, and then release your
forward hand to the ground, while
resting your fore-arm on your mid-thigh.
Extend your opposite arm over your
ear, with your palm facing down.
Position your gaze upwards to your
left hand, if possible.

FOUR LIMBED STAFF POSTURE

*Caution: This pose requires stability and
strong abdominal strength

Begin in a plank pose, adjust your weight
in a way that make your shoulders
slightly ahead your wrists. Bend your
elbows in a 90 degrees position and
press your upper arms into your body
(ensure that your arms are aligned with

your body). Your forearms should be perpendicular to the ground as your chest remains broad. Lastly, strongly begin to engage your abdominals to keep your body in a plank pose.

HALF BOAT POSE

Begin in a boat pose position, and bring your hands to a prayer position. Rest on your bum; raise your upper body and legs lower a few inches from the ground. Lastly, strongly begin to engage your abdominals section.

HAPPY BABY POSE

Lie on your back as you bend your knees,
reaching for the outer edges of your feet.
When you get hold of them, draw them
and the tailbone downward. Now
position the soles of your feet towards
the sky, with the shims perpendicular
to the ground. Option: you can as well
rock sideways like a baby.

HEAD-TO-KNEE POSE

Begin by sitting on the floor, with
your legs stretched out in front of
you, and your back and legs at a
90-degree angle. Now draw in your
right knee towards the groin and
then release your knee to the floor,
with your foot flush against your inner
thigh. Lastly, bend forward to hold your
ankle or foot.

HEADSTAND

Caution: do not attempt this, if you have any neck or shoulder conditions.

Begin by interlacing your hands, with your palm
heels pressed together. Nestle the crown of
your head on the ground between the "v"
of your forearms. Walk your feet towards
your head. Engage the abdominals and pelvic
floor muscles to float your legs towards the sky.
Now use your forearms to mainly maintain
balance, with less pressure on the neck and head.

OPEN ANGLE POSE

Begin this pose in a seated position.
Now straddle your legs very widely,
ensuring that your toes are positioned
towards the sky. Elevate your spine from
the ground and leave it as such. Now try
to fold between your legs. Lastly,
maintain a resting position with your
forearms or on the ground, with your arms outstretched.

PIGEON POSE

Begin in a plank position, and then
move your tight shim directly behind
your hands (parallel to the top of
your mat). Dorsiflex your ankle in order
to protect your knee. (Draw the toes
toward the knee). Now release your
back leg to the ground, energetically
reaching your toes backward. To deepen
this pose, drop your forearms or release
your body to the ground, with your arms
stretched forward.

PLOW POSE

Caution: do not attempt this, if you have a neck condition.

Begin in a seated, and then tuck in your
 navel as you roll onto your back.
 Raise your legs, across your head
and send them across your back,
 till your toes land on the floor.
 Support your lower back, or press
the arms down on the ground.

RECLINING BOUND ANGLE POSE

Begin by lying on your back, and then
press the soles of your feet together
 with your knees pointed outward.
Note that your knees may not readily
 touch easily; if that is the case, place
pillows or blocks underneath to support
them. You can stretch backwards or rest
 your arms on your belly.

SEATED SPINAL TWIST

The first step is to sit on the floor, and
 then extend your legs in front of you,
with your back and legs at a 90-degree
 angle. Now cross your right foot to the
outside of your left knee, and plant your
 foot on the ground. Option: Bend
your left knee in such a way that makes
your foot outside the right hip. Then wrap
your left arm around the bent knee.

SHOULDERSTAND

**Caution: do not attempt this, if you
have a neck condition.**

Sit on the floor, tuck in your navel, and
 gradually roll onto your back. Now raise
 and position your legs and torso
towards the sky. Lastly, support your
lower back with your hands or press your
 hands down on the ground.

STANDING FORWARD BEND

Begin this in a standing position, with
your feet together or hip-width apart.
Maintain a lengthened spine by bending
forward. Now place your hands flat on the
ground, or hold them behind the ankles
to deepen your posture.

SUPPORTED CHILD'S POSE

This is a very unique pose. Begin by
using pillows or bolsters beneath your
body to deepen the comfort of the
Child's Pose. Relax and rest.

SUPPORTED CORPSE POSE

Apart from pillows and bolsters, this
pose might require that you make
use of more materials, such as sandbags,
thick clothes etc. The idea of this is to
deepen the comfort of Corpse Pose—on
areas such as knees, lower back,
wrists, head, or on your belly. If you are
cosy, get a blanket to keep warm,
so that you can rest comfortably.

SUPPORTED FORWARD BEND

As usual, begin the process in a
comfortable position, with your arms
at your sides, and your palms flat on
the floor. Now stretch your legs before
you, ensuring that your toes are positioned
towards the sky. Now bend forward
over a large bolster or pillow as you
allow your whole upper body to relax.

TREE POSE

Begin in a standing position as you rest
your weight on your right foot. Now
float your left leg up, and place it on
the right inner thigh, with your toes
pointing in a downward position.
Finally, place your hands in a position
and rest it at your heart centre.

TRIANGLE POSE

Begin in a standing position as you spread
your arms wide with the feet parallel
3-4 feet apart. Now turn your right foot
out 90 degrees, and look over the right
hand's middle finger. Stretch out far right,
and drop your hand on your shin or on
the ground. Then stretch out your left
hand in a skyward position. Stack hips
positioned above the other.

WARRIOR I

Begin in a standing position as you
stretch your feet hip-width apart.
Step your left feet backwards 4-5 feet
and plant your foot on the ground
(ensure that your toes turned out 30-45
degrees). Now sink your right knee 90
degrees. Broaden your shoulders and hips
forward. Now smoothly sweep your
arms up, with both palms facing each

other. Maintain a neutral spine as you position your gaze towards your hands and heart facing the sky.

WARRIOR 2

Begin in a standing position as you spread your arms, with the feet parallel 4-5 feet apart. Turn your right foot 90 degrees, and sink the front-facing knee to a 90-degree angle. Bring your left foot forward and plant it on the floor as your other leg remains straight. Now position your gaze over the middle finger of your right hand, as you keep your spine erect.

SUN SALUTATION

Stand tall, inhale and raise your arms. Exhale,
and bend forward over, stretching out your
legs and focusing your gaze on your hands
and shins. Now exhale, and get yourself in
a plank position—lowering your knees, chest,
and chin to the ground. Next inhale, and
move into the Cobra or Upward Facing Dog.
Exhale, and move into Downward Facing Dog.
As you do that, stay a while and take up to
five breaths. Again, inhale, and step or
jump your feet between your hands. Exhale
into Standing Forward Fold. Inhale, stand tall,
and raise your arms. Exhale, and bring your
hands to your sides or to prayer position.

CRYSTALS

AMBER

Amber is actually a great stone
used to strengthen the potentials
of the sacral plexus and solar plexus
chakras. It is more beneficial for
the solar plexus chakra, if the hue
gets more yellow; and, more beneficial
for the sacral plexus chakra, if the
hue gets more orange.

AMETHYST

This is unique in such a way that it
is usually the first stones that people
are attracted to, when learning about
crystals. It has a calming aura, and
helps us to cultivate our intuition,
and prevents against psychic attack.
Also, it corresponds to the third eye chakra.

APOPHYLLITE

The appophyllite is known for clearing
 blockages in the crown chakra.
This basically because it corresponds to
the same chakra and equally helps us
 improves our psychic abilities. It appears
 colourless, white or gray; but, sometimes,
 appears in a rare green hue.

AQUAMARINE

Aquamarine is a powerful stone, which
 is blue in colour, and corresponds to
 the throat chakra. It helps us to
improve our communication skills,
 and has a soothing and calming effect
 on the body.

BLACK TOURMALINE

This is a very powerful stone known
 for its grounding nature. It is equally
 for being the premiere stone for
psychic protection as it deflects all
negative energies directed towards
you. It corresponds to the root chakra.
Also, it should be worn on the body.

BLOODSTONE

This is another stone that corresponds
to the root chakra known for its
effective grounding nature. This entails
that it is a stone of vitality, endurance
and strength. Its colour is light green,
with sprinkles of red spots and blotches.

BLUE KYANITE

Blue kyanite is not just known for
corresponding to the throat chakra;
but, for its high vibration capacity.
It also helps the third eye chakra since
it opens up the psychic channels. Its
body can easily be marked by flat,
blade-like striations.

CARNELIAN

This stone is orange in colour, and it
activates the sacral plexus chakra.
Its unique disposition allows it to have
a direct influence on other chakras. If it
has a dark red hue to it, it addresses the
root chakra; but, if it has yellower tones,
it then resonates with the solar plexus chakra.

CELESTITE

This stones often varies in colour, but its most consistent colour is grey-blue. It is effective for contacting or relating with spiritual beings e.g. angels. It not just activates the throat chakra; but, heals other chakras such as the crown and third eye chakras.

CLEAR QUARTZ

The clear quartz stone is popular for its multi-purpose nature in healing or addressing chakras. However, it strength lies more in healing the crown chakra. Another key thing about it is that it amplifies the energy of other chakras to maximise their healing productivity.

CORAL (RED)

The coral crystal comes in various colours;
but, here we would be looking at the red
 one, which activates the root chakra.
 Other functions it performs includes:
 aiding to release impurities from our
muscular system, stimulates our metabolic
processes, strengthens the circulatory
 system and bones in the body.

EMERALD

Emerald is a powerful known for its
strong heart healing capabilities on
 physical and emotional levels. It is one
 of the fewest stones that represent the
 core energy patterns of the activated heart
 chakra. Other functions it performs include:
stimulation of love, compassion,
 healing and abundance.

FLUORITE

Fluorite is another unique crystal.
 It exists in various colours, with even multiple colours of the same
specimen. Regardless, all shades
of it are notably instrumental to
improving mental health problems.
It is related with
 the third eye chakra. And, despite
the varying colours, it heals all chakras.

FIRE AGATE

Fire Agate is a multi-coloured stone,
which has a brown base hue with flashes
 of orange, red, green and gold. It
equally heals a couple of chakras.
 First, it is mostly associated with the
 root chakra; but, it also stimulates the
 solar plexus and sacral plexus chakras.

GARNET

Garnet is another colourful stone, which
 comes with various colours, but is
 consistently red, which associates it is
 the root chakra. It is known for its unique
capacity to cleanse or purify our lives
 of accumulated toxicities. It is also
used in treatment of blood, spine and bone.

GREEN CALCITE

Green calcite also comes in many colours,
but it's most consistent colour is green,
which stimulates the heart chakra.
Its functions include: clearing the heart
chakra of stress, and provides a
conducive atmosphere for enhanced
relaxation, emotional balance and
connection with the heart to occur.

GREEN KYANITE

Green Kyanite is green in colour, and
forms flat, blade-like crystals around
its body. It is another unique crystal that
connects us to our heart chakra. One of
its major functions is to help us find the
truth of our hearts and guiding us to live
from that truth. Note: Do not clean with
salt to avoid damage.

IOLITE

Iolite is a multi-coloured stone, but often
appears as violet, or clear bluish-lavender.
It is associated with the throat, third eye
and crown chakras simply because it opens
up the light pathway from the throat to the
crown chakras. It is known for its
effectiveness in shalamanic journeying and
healing old wounds.

JADE

Jade equally comes in variety of colours;
but then, the green is the most popular and
consistent. The Green jade is highly
instrumental for the balancing and
harmonization of the heart chakra. It is also
a stone for balancing the heart chakra.
 It also creates an atmosphere for the
fostering steady growth of life force energy,
otherwise known as qi.

KUNZITE

Kunzite is a precious crystal that resonates
with the crown and heart chakras.
One of its key functions is to align the
energy of the heart with the mind. It also
opens the heart to the energies of love.
Other functions include: grounding our
beliefs, enhancing our intuition and
helping us lift our confusion.

KYANITE

Kyanite also exists in different colours,
which interestingly render healing
and balance to all the chakras. The
blue-coloured kyanite corresponds with
the throat and third eye chakras, while
the green-coloured kyanite corresponds
with the heart chakra.

LABRADORITE

Labradorite is a unique crystal that has a
touch of many colours in one, such as
green, orange, blue, orange, red, gold
and violet. It is popularly known as the
gemstone of magic. It aids in healing all
other chakras; but, it is more associated
with the crown chakra. Our innate abilities
and creative potentials are enhanced,
when we wear it.

223

LAPIS LAZULI

This particular stone is associated with the throat and third eye chakras, and consequently activates them. Its colours include deep blue, gold and oftentimes, white flecks. It is popularly known and used for clairvoyance and precognition. People seek for it, when they want to have an idea about what is yet to come. If you want to make use of it, place it on your third eye chakra, and you will receive insight and revelation about your dreams.

LEPIDOLITE

Lepidolite resonates with all the chakras; but, activates the heart and third eye chakras. It is a remarkable stone for stimulating serenity and spiritual purification. Therefore, meditating with it would clear blocked energies in all the chakras. It often appears purplish or pink in colour.

LODESTONE

Lodestone is not a crystal; but, a form
of magnetite. It stands out easily, because
it is easily covered with magnetite and
other forms of magnetic materials.
Its key functions include strengthening
the circulatory system and helping to
ameliorate blood disorders. Lastly,
it grounds the root chakra.

MOONSTONE

Moonstone appears, like a blue-white
sheen. It also stimulates the crown
chakra. It is known for its spiritual
capacity to reveal to women their
feminine power and connection to the
goddess. On the part of males, it stimulates
the right side of the brain.

OBSIDIAN

Out of all varieties of obsidian crystals,
 black obsidian is the most common of them
all, which comes in a black, glossy colour.
 It is known for its protective nature,
and also cleanses the auric field of
 disharmony. Most importantly, it grounds
the root chakra, and powerfully eliminates
 negative energies within ourselves
and our environment.

ONYX

The onyx has few varieties; but, the black
 onyx stands out the most. It actually
 grounds the root chakra, and when we
eventually use it, we are deeply grounded
into the electromagnetic energy of the earth.
One of its key functions is to heal our anxieties
by condensing the excessive energies that
 we have accumulated over time.

ORANGE TOURMALINE

Like the aforementioned crystals, tourmaline
 comes in various colours and variations.
It is actually very rare, and often occurs in red
and yellow colours. However, the orange
 tourmaline plays a very key role in the sacral
 plexus chakra by activating it. This further leads
to the improvement of our creativity, sexuality
and intuition of the physical plane.

PERIDOT

The various colours of peridot include gold,
lemon, olive, lime, green etc. It
 balances the heart chakra, as well as
 the solar plexus chakra.
 This consequently improves our ability to
receive Universal Love, which eventually
opens us up to abundance on every side.

PHENACITE

Phenacite is a unique mineral; but, it
can be mistaken for other stones,
such as quartz or topaz, with which it
 shares some physical properties. It
 activates the crown and third eye
chakras. It is also notable for generating
Pure White Light energy.

RED JASPER

The red jasper activates the root chakra,
and as such, firmly grounds us to the
earth. Also, the frequency of this
stone can stimulate someone's kundalini
energy. **Note:** Raising of the kundalini
energy should be done gradually.

ROSE QUARTZ

The rose quartz stone is one of the most
powerful and popular stones out there.
It is regarded as the premiere love
stone. As a matter of fact, it activates
our heart chakra, and improves our
ability to tap into love for others in the
community, our lives, the Earth, the
Universe, the Divine, and our
knowledge of self-love. This is a lot!
When it comes to healing our hearts,
the process is gentle, gradual, but powerful.

RUBY

Ruby is a precious stone, known its
role in stimulating the root chakra,
and infusing great life force and vitality

into our beings. Wearing the ruby
is a valid way to activate your
physical, mental and
emotional bodies.

RUTILATRED QUARTZ

Rutilated quartz is popularly known
for helping to stabilise emotional and
mental processes. Another key function
performs is that it helps to stabilize the
digestive system and improve nutrient
absorption. The rutilated quartz is really
associated with all chakras; but, it mostly
activates the solar plexus chakra.

SELENITE

Selenite easily resonates with the
third eye and crown chakras. It
effectively cleans up the auric
field. Also, it is suitable for wiping
off unwanted energies.

SMOKY QUARTZ

The smoky quartz functions as a
powerful grounding and clearing stone.
As a matter of fact, it not only activates
and opens the smoky quartz; it is equally
known for clearing the aura and energetic
systems. When it comes to grounding,
it absorbs and transmutes negative energy.

SODALITE

Sodalite is a deep blue-coloured, which
 activates the third eye and throat
chakras. Some of its key functions
 include helping us to speak our truths
and highly improve our communication
skill. By so doing, we learn cultivate the
ability to be more positive than negative.
 Issues like sore throat, neck pain, tight
tongue etc. could be resolved by
 using sodalite.

STAR SAPPHIRE

The star sapphire is a unique stone
which is widely known as a stone that
brings good luck and wisdom. It also
activates the third eye chakra, and of
course, improves the balancing of our
thoughts. **Note:** If you want to feel its
effects, meditate with it
over your third eye.

SUGILITE

Sugilite activates the third eye and
crown chakras in a powerful way.
Interestingly, it is an amazing stone
known for its numerous unique qualities.
It boosts our spirits to be confident in
situations that threaten our motivation
or shrink us to hopelessness. It is protective,
purifying and activates our
hearts and minds.

SUNSTONE

The name of this crystal is derived from
its physical properties, such as its
warm colour and reflected light, which
reminds us of the sun. It is known for
stimulating creativity and sexuality in
us. Lastly, it energizes the sacral plexus
and solar plexus chakras.

TANZANITE

Tanzanite appears in various shades of
hue; but, the most common of them al
l appear in blue, blue-violet, golden,
brownish and yellow. It activates the
third eye and crown chakras. Also, it
helps us to stay centred in wisdom by
integrating the energies of our
minds and hearts.

TURQUOISE

Turquoise is said to be about the longest-used
of all gemstones on earth. One unique thing
about it is that it is a stone of forgiveness.
Also, it resonates with the root chakra, and
wearing it empowers us with courage and boldness
to share and impact our world with our purpose.

WHITE TOPAZ

White topaz is equally referred to
"colourless topaz" due its colourless
or glassy outlook. It resonates with the
crown, which, in turn, helps us to improve
our psychic and intuitive abilities. It is also
known for its ability to help those who are
scared to tell the truth to do so effectively.

YELLOW AGATE

Yellow agate balances the solar plexus chakra.
This has many health benefits, like aiding
digestive issues, such as food allergies and
metabolism, and improving concentration
and memory. It also equips us with the
capacity to cultivate self-confidence,
strength and courage.

YELLOW CITIRINE

Citrine comes in various shades of hue
such as pale, yellow, gold and sometimes,
brown. It is known for powerfully purifying
our centre. Also, it stimulates the solar plexus
chakra, and strengthens our will.

YELLOW TIGER'S EYE

Yellow tiger's eye is a unique stone which basically stimulates the third eye chakra. When this occurs, we receive support in handling our challenges, without being thrown off in the process. Also, it is widely known as stone for vitality, practicality, mental clarity and physical action.

YELLOW TOPAZ

Yellow topaz appears in yellow, gold or brown sometimes. It resonates with the solar plexus chakra, and when activated helps us to manifest our life's aspirations. Also, it serves as a tool for effective relaxation, rest and calming stress. **Note:** It is worn on the body, when in use.

CPSIA information can be obtained
at www.ICGtesting.com
Printed in the USA
LVHW101624261022
731628LV00005B/251